An APPALACHIAN TRIAL

A Story of Struggle, Survival,
and God's Grace

DANIEL LIPSI

WESTBOW
PRESS®
A DIVISION OF THOMAS NELSON
& ZONDERVAN

WestBow Press books may be ordered through booksellers or by contacting:

WestBow Press
A Division of Thomas Nelson & Zondervan
1663 Liberty Drive
Bloomington, IN 47403
www.westbowpress.com
1 (866) 928-1240

ISBN: 978-1-5127-8674-3 (sc)
ISBN: 978-1-5127-8675-0 (hc)
ISBN: 978-1-5127-8673-6 (e)

Library of Congress Control Number: 2017907621

Print information available on the last page.

WestBow Press rev. date: 05/18/2017

Dedicated to my wife, Donna, my children,
Charis, Dorea, and Nathan, and to my grandchildren,
Valerie and Joshua, and most recently, Abigail Jean

To the Glory of God

TABLE OF CONTENTS

FOREWORD

I met Dan Lipsi in college where we both studied engineering. Our course work was challenging, so there was a real sense of camaraderie among those of us in the program. Dan and I came to discover we were both Christians back then, and both of us were active in our respective churches. But honestly, we were more focused on our education and career paths, than in pursuing a deeper friendship. After graduation, we lost touch for a few years. Dan had moved into a position in the family business, a manufacturing company that produced industrial heat treating furnaces, and I went on to pursue religious studies after a short career in engineering. All of that happened about 10 years before the events described here in *An Appalachian Trial*.

Our paths, however, crossed again about twenty years later when I accepted a call to serve as pastor of the church where I discovered Dan and his family happened to be members. We resumed what had been until then a casual friendship, and it deepened as we served the Lord together. Today, more than twenty-five years later, our connection is strong. Now we are both in the stage of our lives when we are considering what our legacy will be and how our lives will be remembered, especially by those closest to us. Being diligent providers and faithful family men is certainly important. But we long for our lives to count for more; we want our loved ones to know that there were times when we encountered God when we needed him most. We understand the desire of the Psalmist's heart when he pleaded, "Even when I am old and gray, do not forsake me, O God, until I declare your power to the next generation, your might to all who are to come." (Psalm 71:18, NIV) Can we dare to expect to find God's mercy and faithfulness when we are helpless and nearly hopeless? This account represents Dan's testimony of this experience and desire in his life.

I still remember standing on a mountain side in Virginia one spring, near the site of Dan's *Appalachian Trial*, as Dan related to me the broad brushstrokes of the story that unfolds here in greater detail. It was a deeply moving story then, and it is only intensified by the details. In this re-telling of his story, Dan has taken the time to reflect on what he learned about himself, and what he learned about the God who never left his side. This is a story about what takes place when happenstance and human error intersect with the sovereignty of God.

By the way, it is also my happy privilege to know Peter, Janet, Marion, and of course, Donna. Their insights are especially enriching and encouraging. It is good to remember that when we go through personal struggles others often share the tragedy and triumph with us. So in many respects this is a story about the people who shared this personal crisis with Dan. And not only family, but trail hikers, EMTs, ICU nurses, pilots and pastors that helped Dan in his hour of need. But it is clear that it was God that brought those people across Dan's path. How wonderful is God's providential care! Ultimately, this is a story about indefatigable hope, unfailing love and abundant grace – because it's a story about how God cares for His own in the trials of life.

Rev. James B. Camlin
Pastor, Montgomery Baptist Church

As a missionary home on furlough in the 1960s I looked forward to visiting the Lipsi home in Colmar, PA. Tony and Jean Lipsi loved missionaries. The welcome mat was always out for those who served the Lord in some distant land. Hospitality was part of Jean's DNA. She used every opportunity God gave her to put her gift of hospitality to work. And Tony was equally engaged. God had blessed Tony and his business and they shared God's blessings generously. Their home with all its amenities was available to those serving the Lord. Sitting around the pool, eating specially prepared dinners and desserts prepared by Jean and having great conversations about what God was doing around the world was a blessing beyond description to returning missionaries.

It was during our first furlough from Peru that I met their son Dan. I had been invited to speak at their church, Montgomery Baptist, and was hosted for the weekend at the Lipsi home. For the next twenty years, every four years, we would look forward to reporting to Montgomery Baptist and reconnecting with the Lipsi family, and it was a large one. Tony and Jean had six children and Dan was second in the birth order. At the time of my first visit, he was only eleven or twelve years old but he would sit attentively and listen to my stories about flying missionaries into remote locations where the gospel had never gone before.

Over the years, Dan developed his own interest in aviation and, after graduating from college, got his pilot's license. He told me that, upon earning his first paycheck and buying his first car, the next thing he did after graduating was sign up for flying lessons at a local airport.

My association with Montgomery Baptist Church, the Lipsi family, and with Dan has been a rewarding one. There is a special bond that is formed when two pilots have opportunity to fly together. Dan and I had several opportunities over the years, on trips that included traveling to evaluate a possible aircraft purchase for JAARS, traveling to Wycliffe USA board meetings in Georgia, and some recreational flights in California. Dan also flew his own plane to the JAARS base in Waxhaw, North Carolina on several occasions during my time of service there to work on various projects such as pouring concrete floor in a new T-hanger, constructing and hanging doors on the same hanger and helping us with a renovation project in our home.

Tony and Jean took seriously God's instructions to "train up a child in the way he should go and when he is old he will not depart from it." Dan is an example of just that. The things I so admired in his parents are characteristics I see in Dan and they come through in his book.

In this book, Dan shares his story of how, at critical moments in his life, God shows up. This is true for all those who follow Him. It has certainly been true for me.

I commend this book to you and trust God blesses you through its reading.

Bernie May
Founder- The Seed Company, Former President- Wycliffe Bible Translators, US, Former Executive Director- JAARS, Missionary Pilot/Mechanic

PREFACE

If you are one of my children, grandchildren, nieces, or nephews, I wrote this story for you. If you are one of my siblings or one of my many cousins, I wrote this story for you. But perhaps, you are not a member of my family. Perhaps you are a person who now finds yourself in a dark place in life where God seems very far away, disinterested, or unapproachable. Perhaps you even feel like you've put yourself in this place; you feel that you are responsible for whatever predicament you are in and, because of that, you feel you are beyond God's help. You have convinced yourself you are only getting what you deserve. If you are that person, I wrote this story for you too.

The events of this story began on November 20, 1978, the day before the accident that took the life of my brother, John Mark Lipsi—Mark, to his friends and family. Our parents took his name directly from Scripture. Our Mark was the namesake of the John Mark we know from the New Testament, author of the Gospel of Mark. That John Mark also used his middle name with those who knew him. My parents followed this precedent.

John Mark Lipsi—Mark, to everyone who knew him.

For those in our extended family who did not live through this chapter of our history, you may have heard bits and pieces of the story and you probably know that you had an uncle or cousin named Mark who passed away, perhaps before you were born. You may have heard enough, often enough, to realize this story has lurked in the background shadows of our family ever since it unfolded. I lived it, yet even I was mildly surprised to learn from a sibling that the details of the story are still a topic of conversation between my brother and all my sisters. This conversation continues from time-to-time now, almost thirty-seven years after the events. Each of my siblings had their own perspective on the events and their own story, and they continued to have their own questions. I was told that, since Pete was on the scene shortly after the accident, he was the information source for my sisters. Yet, to them, he seemed as obsessed with the details and timeline as any of them were. Ironically, I wasn't included in any of these conversations, and I never fully realized just how many questions have lingered over the decades.

I have only recently managed to get the events down on paper. It's not that I hadn't tried before. Over the years, I made several aborted attempts but was never able to force myself to follow through to completion for one reason or another. So why now, after several failed attempts over almost thirty-seven years, did I find enough motivation to stay with the project and follow it through to completion? I can only say that the time felt right. I thought I needed to act now or this story would disappear with me, and I would have lost a great opportunity to share a gift with all the members of our extended family. I knew I wasn't getting any younger. I knew this chapter of our family's history had profound consequences on who we are and how we function as a family, and I learned that my own siblings still had questions. I knew that, while bits and pieces of the story may have been passed down to our children and grandchildren, that's all they had ever heard—bits and pieces.

Most importantly, however, I knew this story was really the story of God's grace in my life and in our family's. I wanted our children and grandchildren to know about it and have the opportunity to internalize it. It is emphasized in Scripture, especially in the Old Testament, that the generation who saw and experienced the direct hand of God operating in their lives was instructed to pass this firsthand knowledge of God's activity on to the succeeding generations in verbal, written, and memorialized form. Certainly I should attempt to do the same thing. I had first-hand experience to pass on.

Finally, to anyone who reads this account, please be assured that I do not think I was called upon to suffer to any extraordinary degree. On the contrary, I consider the burden of these events to be light compared to what some others are called to bear. Every family experiences loss at some time in their history; we are not unique in that respect. I do think, however, we were extraordinarily blessed to have seen the hand of God working in our lives in what I believe were miraculous ways. I want God to get any glory. Certainly none belongs to me.

Dan Lipsi

February, 2015

INTRODUCTION

I had recently contacted a cousin through social media to whom I had not spoken in several years. His simple greeting to me was, "How are you doin', Danny?" My reply to him was equally simple. "Better than I deserve!"

That response can be a flippant reply to a rhetorical greeting or it can actually be a serious answer that is true on a number of levels. Admittedly, I had already heard the same answer from several people I know and I just borrowed it. But it is no coincidence that I knew most of the others to be committed Christians—people who profess a relationship with the living Christ and who testify to His active presence in their lives. This is my own story and it illustrates just how much my answer is true, in both a physical and spiritual sense.

CHAPTER 1

THE CALL

*T*he call came in to the office shortly after lunch on a Monday in November, three days before Thanksgiving. My father took the call; it was from an out-of-state customer complaining about his tool room heat treat furnace. He claimed his furnace wasn't operating properly. He wanted service and he wanted it now.

My father had founded the family business in 1959. It was an industrial equipment manufacturing operation. We designed and fabricated high-temperature industrial furnaces and ovens that were used for various metal heat-treat operations and thermal processing. I had been working in the business, unofficially since I was twelve years old and officially, as a full-time employee on the payroll, since my graduation from college some seven years prior. My younger brother Mark also worked in the business as a full-time employee, beginning immediately after his high school graduation. His full-time status actually preceded mine by two years. Peter, my youngest brother, did not work in the family business at that time. He was employed as a skilled woodworker and craftsman, building high-end furniture, antique reproductions, hand-carved relief paneling and art objects for well-heeled clients at a local wood crafting shop.

Cessna 175 Skylark- Ours was equipped with a 215HP
6-cylinder Franklin engine and constant speed prop
yielding a cruise speed of 155 mph. (photo used by
permission from www.AirTeamImages.com).

Dad tried to be diplomatic. He suggested to the caller we could fulfill the service-call request after the Thanksgiving holiday. However, this customer was unwilling to accept that offer. He insisted only an immediate service call would do—and now he wanted it "yesterday." Inconveniently for us, the customer was in North Carolina, in the Durham area, and we were in Pennsylvania. In the hope of getting there and back before Thanksgiving Day, Mark and I decided we would fly there in the small four-place single-engine aircraft that I owned jointly with the business. We packed up our service gear and left the shop. Mark still lived in our parents' home so he went there to pack his personal belongings for the trip. I remember also going to my parents' house before going to my own home to pack my gear, but the reason for that intermediate stop escapes me now. After collecting our personal gear, we joined up again at the airport where our plane was kept.

CHAPTER 2

FLYING SOUTH

I was a fairly low-time private pilot who was qualified for VFR (visual flight rules) flight only. Essentially, this meant I could only legally fly if the reported ceiling was one thousand feet or more AGL (above ground level) and the reported visibility was three statute miles or greater along my intended route of flight. Other restrictions also applied. The cloud clearance requirements of VFR flight meant I could not legally penetrate a solid overcast layer to fly at a higher altitude in clear air, nor should I fly at an altitude closer than five hundred feet below the base of the overcast cloud layer. There were also restrictions to available altitudes based on the direction of flight. I did have experience in cross-country flying despite my relatively limited total time as pilot-in-command. I had also flown into that part of the country several times before. I was approved for night flying and met the currency requirements for legal night flight.

The preflight weather briefing for that night indicated exceptionally good weather conditions for the flight—always good news for a VFR-only rated pilot. By the time we had packed, planned the flight, received a weather briefing, and completed the standard preflight inspection, it was 4:30 p.m. It would be dark in less than an hour. Just before heading to the airport, I had said goodbye to my wife, Donna, who was three months pregnant with our first child. I told her after we completed our service call, we might continue further south to Waxhaw, North Carolina, to the JAARS Center (Jungle Aviation and Radio Service) to pay a visit to some family friends. JAARS is the support, technical, communication, and aviation branch of a missionary organization, Wycliffe Bible Translators. The actual time of our return was left in doubt. It might be Tuesday night. It might be Wednesday night.

Significantly, before this service-call flight came up, I was scheduled to take the FAA Instrument Rating Written Examination on the Friday immediately after Thanksgiving. This is a requirement for earning an Instrument Rating as a private pilot and I was determined to earn this advanced rating to expand my flying capability. So for this flight, I decided to take my Jeppesen Low Altitude Enroute Charts and one binder of approach plates. I thought it would be a good opportunity to get some actual flying experience using them. I did have my VFR sectional charts in my flight case, but they remained there for the entire duration of this trip.

There is a big difference between the two types of enroute charts. Jeppesen Low Altitude Enroute Charts are packed with the information required to fly in controlled airspace using the national air traffic control system in weather where flight is accomplished solely by reference to the aircraft instruments and with no visual contact with the ground (except for the very last part of a landing approach). Consequently, there are no topographical renderings on the charts. VFR sectional charts are quite different in that they are multicolored charts that clearly depict topographical terrain complete with color coding and contour line markings. Overlaid on the terrain is the airspace navigation information that can be used by VFR pilots. These charts depict terrain information because they are intended to be used for VFR flight that requires reference and sight lines to the ground.

We took off into a clear late-afternoon sky with virtually unlimited visibility and minimum wind. It was a beautiful night to fly with virtually no turbulence. Conditions were ideal as darkness descended over the late-autumn landscape smoothly passing beneath us. It was wonderful to fly in conditions like this. Even though the plane was not equipped with auto-pilot, the plane stayed on course and at the desired altitude with minimal control inputs due to the complete lack of turbulence. As I flew I remembered another similar night flight I had made just a week before getting married two years prior. Ironically, I had flown on the reverse course I was on now as I had been returning home from another business trip. On that night the air had been absolutely silky smooth, but the visibility had been near minimums due to humidity and haze as opposed to clouds. Because of the limited visibility on that extended cross-country night flight, it had felt like I was ensconced in a dark cocoon. I had been barely connected to the earth in any way, suspended in my own little universe. Only the instrument needles that quivered slightly with engine vibration had given me a sense I was in a real airplane and not a simulator. Flying is magic in benign night conditions like that.

Mark, as the bagel maker.

The approximately three-and-a-half hour flight progressed without incident, and little conversation passed between my brother and I; he seemed engrossed in his own thoughts and I was engrossed in aviating.

As we approached our destination, the Raleigh-Durham Airport, I took a few minutes to study the airport layout depicted in my charts because I would be flying into this large, controlled, commercial airport for the first time, and I'd be doing it at night. It had been my experience that orienting myself to the overall layout of the airport while in flight was easy compared to navigating it on the ground. Large airports can be very confusing on the ground at night if you are not familiar with them. If I needed to, I was going to ask ground control for "progressive taxi instructions" to make sure I did not end up somewhere I did not belong once we were on the ground. Asking for progressive taxi instructions can be problematic if the airport surface traffic is busy and the ground controllers are occupied. It increases their work load significantly. Requesting progressive taxi instructions is asking the ground controller to continually watch your every move on the airport surface and to sequentially issue turn-by-turn instructions as required. Under normal operations, the ground controller issues a complete, overall clearance to the desired ground destination or to an intermediate "hold short" location with a summary of taxiway designations defining the surface route. It is then up to the pilot to carry out those instructions and successfully navigate the labyrinth of runways and taxiways to arrive at his ground destination or the clearance limit.

As we came within twenty miles of the airport I monitored the ATIS (automatic terminal information service) frequency, a recorded loop transmitted continuously, and learned the wind direction, speed, visibility, local altimeter setting, and the runway in use. Fifteen miles from the airport, I raised approach control on the radio to let them know our VFR flight was inbound for landing. They assigned a transponder code, and I was positively identified on the approach controller's radar screen. I was then slotted and vectored for a visual approach to runway Thirty-Two-Right. After receiving radar vectors (turn and heading instructions issued by the radar approach controller) and becoming established on a left downwind track for the runway in use, I was handed off to the control tower for final instructions and clearance to land.

Another beautiful sight every pilot loves to see on a night flight after turning to the final-approach course heading is the array of approach lights leading to a runway at a large airport. A runway's approach light array, runway edge lighting, and center lighting, along with threshold lighting and even VASI lighting (visual approach slope indicator) are simply beautiful to see at night in good weather. It was amazing to realize this long stretch of concrete with all this technology was all mine at that very moment. However, I could not sight-see very long or ponder my privileged vantage point because I had to land an airplane and was soon crossing the runway threshold. I smoothly touched down within the first three hundred feet of runway, rolled out, and then turned left off the runway onto the second taxiway we approached on our roll-out per the instructions from the control tower. Once clear of the active runway and stopped on the taxiway, we were handed off to ground control. I told the ground controller I wanted to taxi to the nearest FBO for overnight parking. I was glad to discover the general aviation parking apron was not far off to our left, and the taxi instructions were simple and straightforward, so I did not need progressive taxi instructions to get there after all. We proceeded per instruction and taxied to a random empty tie-down spot in the general aviation parking area where we shut down, deplaned, and began to unload our gear. An FBO agent met us at the plane, tied it down, and loaded our gear into the station wagon he had driven to our plane. He then drove us to the FBO office that was over one hundred yards away from our parking spot. (fixed base operation—a corporate aviation service provider with facilities on the airport.) There, we registered, ordered fuel for the plane, rented a car, and made a hotel reservation for the night. The FBO agent then drove us to the rental car provider that was located elsewhere on the airport where we bid him goodbye.

Following a half hour drive, we finally arrived at our downtown hotel sometime after ten p.m. that night. It had been a long day. But after getting settled in for the night, Mark and I talked for a long time after we turned out the lights. He had a lot on his mind concerning the direction of his personal life. My brother did not often open up to me about his personal life, and I remember being surprised at his candor and openness as he spoke to me about what was going on and the questions and potential choices he was pondering—along with the potential consequences of whatever option he was mulling over at the moment. We talked for well over an hour before the conversation trailed off as we both eventually drifted off to sleep.

Mark, in a self-portrait.

The next morning, we drove to the customer's factory, got ourselves and our equipment to the job site and began to trouble-shoot his problem. The customer's problem turned out to be—*there was no problem*— at least not with the equipment as we were led to believe. We did, however, discover the customer had installed an unauthorized and dangerous modification to the system control wiring. This modification deactivated an audible alarm and bypassed a key safety system. They apparently over-rode the safety control system because they did not understand why it was there or how it functioned, and to them it became a nuisance. Instead of investigating why this alarm was constantly being activated during furnace operations, they simply disconnected it from the system and actually by-passed a key safety shut-off feature. It became clear to me the real problem stemmed from the operators having an incomplete and inaccurate understanding of the furnace's design and operation. I discovered no one person was in charge of operating this furnace; each of about twenty machinists in the shop was expected to operate the furnace as he needed. None of them had received any training, and apparently, no one had even bothered to read the furnace operating manual we supplied with the equipment.

Once I had spoken to several machinists and felt I understood what was going on, I walked into the tool room manager's office to report on our activity. He had originally placed the service-call request with us and insisted on our immediate response to what became a demand for factory service and support. I explained to him just what was happening in his own shop under his own nose and that he needed to address the operators' lack of training. I also told him he was being charged for this service call as the equipment was operating normally after we removed the unauthorized modification to the control system and restored the furnace to the configuration we originally supplied. By the time I was done laying out the situation, all he could do was shake his head and admit we were right. As far as I was concerned, it was an unwarranted emergency service call request and a major imposition and inconvenience to us. Our trip should not have been required at all. The service call took the entire day.

CHAPTER 3

FLYING HOME

*B*y the time we left the customer, grabbed a meal, drove back to the airport, turned in our car, got to the FBO, loaded the plane, did the preflight check and got a weather briefing, it was approaching eight-thirty p.m. We decided to forgo the visit to JAARS and head straight for home. I had not had the time to call anyone at JAARS to let them know we were even in the area.

The weather briefing I received from Flight Service was unusual in that it was incomplete and not entirely helpful. The Flight Service Meteorologist could only tell me this was due to the teletype service being down in the Northeast. (If you are twenty-five or younger, ask your parents what a "teletype" is.) Flight Service could not provide any current information regarding the flying conditions north of Washington, DC. I did learn, however, conditions up to the Washington area were currently acceptable VMC (visual meteorological conditions—meeting VFR flight rules), but I also learned the ceilings and visibilities were forecasted to be lowering as we headed further north. Reported visibilities, as far as they had them, were acceptable but not great—five to seven miles for the route. I was, therefore, legal to take off and fly because there were VFR conditions for the known route—at least as far as Washington. From there, I would have to get weather information from Flight Service via radio for points north of Washington, DC in order to legally continue the flight. The forecast of lowering ceilings meant that instead of flying *above* Washington's controlled airspace, I'd likely have to fly *through* it, requiring radio contact and clearance from multiple radar approach control facilities along our route of flight. For some reason, I just did not want to deal with that. This far removed from that timeframe, I can only now speculate that I was tired after a long day, so I planned an alternative route I could fly with minimal radio communication requirements. I can only now speculate that I was tired after a long day. In any event, using my Jeppesen charts as reference, I planned an alternate route that avoided Washington's controlled airspace altogether, bypassing it to the west. While this route was less direct and headed toward the rising terrain of the mountains that border the eastern side of the Shenandoah Valley, it required no radio communication or clearances from ATC at all. But it was a route I had never flown before, and consequently, I had never plotted it on my VFR sectional charts to actually study the specific details of the terrain features I would be flying over.

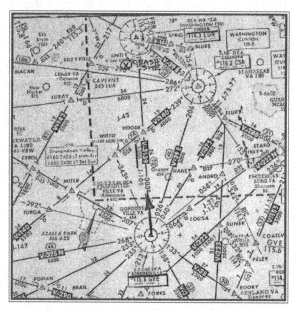

The navigation chart I used was recovered from the crash site by the NTSB. An NTSB investigator added the arrow above the Gordonsville VOR identifier, underlined the MEA and marked the approximate crash location with an "X". (photo used by permission from Jeppesen, A Boeing Company)

Finally, almost exactly at eight-thirty p.m., we were in our plane, belted into our seats, and ready to depart. But then I suddenly realized there was one important detail I had failed to cross off my mental departure check list. I had failed to call home to advise anyone we were on our way. I regretted this oversight because I knew Donna and my parents deserved to be apprised of our revised itinerary. The open-ended nature of the travel plans we had discussed yesterday before our departure, had left our return date in doubt. Nevertheless, I chose not to rectify my omission since reaching a phone at that moment meant deplaning and walking a two-hundred yard roundtrip to the nearest public telephone. And regardless, I expected to be home in less than four hours.

It was Tuesday night, November 21.

As we departed the Raleigh-Durham Airport and climbed out to our cruising altitude and desired heading, I remember listening to the radio chatter between what I assumed was a seasoned professional airline captain on a commercial flight and Raleigh departure control since I was assigned the same radio frequency. This captain was taking some liberties on the departure control frequency to kibitz with the controller handling his flight. This was something I, as a lowly private pilot, would never dare to do, but this captain was probably very well known to the Raleigh controllers and they tolerated and reciprocated the banter as he spoke with a commanding and authoritative but leisurely southern drawl. It must have been a slow night for the controllers and it was amusing as they kidded with one another. But eventually, we were beyond the Raleigh area and navigating on our own on a very dark night with no moon or stars because of the overcast. The visibility, although adequate, was not the brilliantly clear unlimited visibility of the previous night.

Like last night, flying was smooth heading home, yet we could legally fly no higher than 3500 feet MSL (mean sea level) because of a solid overcast between 4000 and 4500 feet MSL. And just as the forecast predicted, I had the sense the ceiling was gradually lowering as we progressed along our route of flight. An hour and a half into the flight, we passed the Washington area to the west as planned. I was flying almost directly north from the Gordonsville VOR (very-high-frequency

12

omnidirectional radio beacon) to the Linden VOR along Victor Airway V3-39. My intention was to call Flight Service for an update on weather conditions further north when I reached the Linden VOR. The MEA (minimum enroute altitude) for this segment of the airway was clearly marked as 5000 feet MSL on the Jeppesen low altitude enroute chart I was using for this portion of the flight. I reasoned the underlying terrain height could not be higher than 3000 feet MSL, because in mountainous terrain, the MEA for a published airway is supposed to provide at least 2000 feet of clearance over the terrain plus be high enough to ensure radio communication and navigation capability over the VHF line-of-sight aviation radio frequencies in use. This was what I thought based on what I had been taught. Flying at 3500 Feet MSL was cutting the margin pretty thin, but I thought at the time it was adequate.

I noticed Mark appeared to be sleeping, inches from my right shoulder. He had adjusted his seat to the maximum rearward position in its floor tracks to give himself as much leg-room as possible and to avoid interfering with the rudder pedals and control wheel that were duplicated in front of the right-side passenger seat where he sat. He was slouched in his seat with his chin on his chest and with his arms folded across his chest. He had unclasped his seat belt in order to slouch down as much as possible. It was approximately ten p.m. or a bit later.

I knew I was getting close to the Linden VOR as the VOR course-deviation indicator in my instrument panel was getting very twitchy with increased sensitivity. I expected the TO/FROM indicator to switch in just a minute or two, indicating station passage. I glanced at my altimeter. It said I was at 3300 feet MSL. With one hand on the primary com radio's frequency selector-knob to change it to the appropriate flight-service com frequency, I simultaneously began to raise the nose of the airplane to regain the two-hundred feet I had deviated from my desired cruising altitude. While hand-flying the airplane, I had allowed it to stray from the desired altitude while my attention was diverted for a few seconds to check my charts for the appropriate flight service radio-communication frequency prior to my call for a weather briefing.

CHAPTER 4

THE CRASH

*S*ilence. Total silence. Only silence and darkness defined my world.

Slowly, impossibly, it began to dawn on me… I did not seem to be flying an airplane anymore. Although, at first, this thought was totally nonsensical to me, I could not mentally reconcile the inconsistency of flying an airplane with the fact that I was surrounded by silence and darkness. How could it be? Was I dreaming? As the mists in my mind slowly evaporated, I realized that instead of sitting in the pilot's seat of my airplane listening to the steady drone of the engine, I seemed to be laying on the leafy, dirt, and boulder-covered terra firma of a silent black world. I was lying face down and fully stretched out with my arms extended downward, parallel to the sides of my body. Before I even moved, I realized my mouth was full of dirt and leaves, and I also became aware my teeth did not line up quite right as I started to work my jaw. I turned my head to one side and began to spit out the dirt and leaves clogging my mouth. I drifted in and out of consciousness while, in this semi-conscious state, a dreamlike image was appearing and re-appearing, playing on a continuous, slow-motion loop in my mind…

I am reaching for the radio frequency-selector knob preparing to make my call to Flight Service for an updated weather briefing when the steady drone of the airplane engine is suddenly interrupted by what sounds like large wet mops slapping against the thin aluminum skin of my airplane. The windscreen in front of my face explodes, shattering into a thousand small pieces of glittering Plexiglas. They strangely whirl in slow motion past my face as I am simultaneously hit by a hurricane-force wind intensifying the chaos unfolding in front of me. The wind screams past my face and ears and the roar like a freight train overpowers all my other senses. My arms flail uncontrollably. I have no control over anything. Something tears the watch from my left wrist but my focus seems strangely drawn to the individual Plexiglas shards glittering and twirling in an illogical slow-motion dance amidst what otherwise is a fierce maelstrom. Then my focus suddenly shifts and I see my brother mysteriously levitate rearward out of his seat. With impossible slowness, he floats rearward toward the back of the plane while simultaneously twisting into a curled, facedown posture. At the same time, the airplane's cabin roof is being peeled backward and is replaced by the blackness of an undefined space. At the very instant Mark reaches the very rear of the cabin and seems about to disappear into the cargo storage area just behind the rear bench-seat, I am catapulted forward into oblivion by some irresistible force. My vision goes dark and the loop ends only to be rewound and replayed in my mind, over and over again...

And there, in total silence and blackness, I gradually began to comprehend: I was reliving the very last second of my flight in very slow motion and in excruciating detail.

CHAPTER 5

MY STRUGGLE

I groggily attempted to raise my head out of the dirt and leaves as my brain started to function at basement level self-awareness; it began to process the information coming in from my environment. My first conscious awareness was the feeling that the forest floor was adhering to my face when I raised my head. I also became aware I could not open my right eye and I could barely see from my left eye with some effort. In the blackness, I seemed to sense shapes rather than see them. And then there was the profound awareness of the absolute, complete, total silence that surrounded me—not a sound of any kind except the slight rustle of leaves created by my own small movements. I viscerally felt the blanketing silence just like anyone who has been in a cave feels the impenetrable blackness; it was enveloping.

Where was the airplane? I was no longer strapped into a seat but was totally free of the airplane. As I lifted my head again, I attempted to push the upper half of my body off the ground to look behind me. My arms seemed to function well enough as I repositioned them to push myself off the ground, but when my spine arched, I began to feel pain for the first time. This sudden sensation of pain jogged my mind out of its groggy, barely-comprehending level of consciousness to a higher level where it was beginning to try and connect the dots. I noted my lower left leg did not want to move in concert with its upper half. And with the small movements I did make, I realized I was feeling the broken ends of my left femur, just above my knee, clicking, grinding and scraping against each other with each movement or exertion. This sensation forced me to concede I had a badly broken left leg, an idea my brain was strangely reluctant to accept at first. My brain also started to process the nature and extent of my facial wound as my right eye refused to open and as I began to mentally focus on the warm sticky blood that was running down my face from above my right eye and dripping from my chin. I continued to spit out as much dirt as I could, my brain again making note of the feeling that none of my teeth seemed to line up quite right, as if a heavy blow to my jaw had changed its alignment. The dots were starting to create a discernible image and I slowly realized, on a completely conscious and rational level, something terrible had happened. As this fully-formed thought coalesced in my brain, I tried to pick off as many of the leaves as I could that were glued to my face. As I gently probed my face it seemed to be a scrambled mess, but I discovered much of what I was feeling were leaves glued to my face by congealing blood.

I managed to turn my head enough to see the shape of the exposed airplane engine almost directly behind me. The engine cowling was completely gone and the exposed engine cylinders were right at ground level. The twisted and bent propeller was still attached to the engine. I was lying about five feet in front of the engine that seemed to still be attached to the engine compartment firewall but at a crazy angle. Beyond that, I could not make out any of the details of the indefinable black shapes I sensed through my squinting left eye. I laid there for an unknown length of time, perhaps hours, slipping in and out of consciousness.

Sometime during this time period, as I laid there, it began to rain—a hard, cold, and steady icy rain—and I was dragged back into the world of consciousness by this frigid shower. In addition to a shirt and slacks, I was wearing only an uninsulated single-layer nylon snap-up jacket over my shirt. I became aware the shoe was missing from my right foot as the toes of that foot were beginning to ache from the cold. It didn't take long to become thoroughly soaked and shivering. To add insult and humiliation to injury, I also had a disgusting feeling; at some point I had lost control of my bowels. The temperature seemed to be dropping through the night and I was unrelentingly chilled by the icy rain that continued to soak me. Now, the only sound I heard was the steady drone of falling rain through higher mostly nude tree branches and the rain dripping from lower branches, so I knew I was completely surrounded by trees. But where? And how close was I to any kind of civilization or help? Early on, when I awoke from unconsciousness, I attempted to cry out for help—mainly because it seemed like that was supposed to be what I should do under the circumstances—not because I expected any help to be nearby. But only a couple of attempts made me realize it took more energy than I could spare, and I quickly gave up after only two brief attempts.

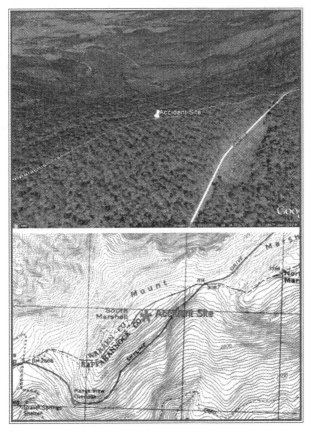

The crash site- satellite image and topo map location. (Google Earth Image Copyright 2016, Google; Topo Map Image Copyright 2016, US Geological Survey)

And then the thought hit me like a boxer's roundhouse to the gut. *My brother. Where was my brother and what had I done to him?* A shudder passed through me that had nothing to do with the cold. Now the idea of getting closer to the wreckage seemed imperative. Maybe he was somewhere tangled in or near the wreckage. The wreckage was behind me but I could not move backward due to my broken leg. As I pondered this conundrum, I realized that only moving forward would keep my leg in slight tension and keep the ends of my broken femur from grinding so forcefully against each other that moving would be painfully intolerable. So in order to reach the wreckage behind me, I had to pull myself forward by arm strength alone in a wide arc to reorient my body to face the wreckage as I inched toward it. I could only move an inch or two at a time and there seemed to be interfering rocks and boulders everywhere. I also needed to frequently stop and rest between attempts to move. But little-by-little over time, I began to make the circle back around to the wreckage, dragging my torso and legs through the tangle of branches, rocks and boulders that seemed to clutch at me as I attempted to move. I tried to stabilize my fractured left leg as best I could by hooking my right foot under my left ankle as I dragged myself along. The rain kept falling, but the exertion created some self-induced heat and I actually felt a bit warmer during this ordeal.

As I was inching forward, attempting to turn left in an arcing path, I came across the airplane tow bar lying on the ground directly in my path.

The tow bar was a telescoping tubular steel implement carried as equipment in the plane. It had a handle at one end and a socketed spring-loaded clamping mechanism at the opposite end designed to engage the steering lug extensions of the airplane nose wheel axle. After the engine was shut off, the tow bar could be manually attached to the nose wheel steering lugs, to provide leverage to turn the nose wheel as the plane was manually maneuvered and aligned into a parking position.

I thought the tow bar would be useful as a splint because the clamping end was shaped like a closed-ended wishbone where I could place my foot and the handle was extendable to about three feet. As I continued to inch along, I also eventually glimpsed a fleece-lined short jacket I had carried in the airplane. It was lying six or seven feet beyond me. The jacket had been lying on the rear seat of the plane but now it was the furthest item I could see in front of the airplane wreckage. I was able to extend my arms and the fully extended tow bar just far enough to hook the jacket to pull it toward me. I was careful to bring the jacket and tow bar with me as I slowly inched around my arc to go back to the wreckage.

I have no idea how long it took to move around the circle to where I could see more of the wreckage, but once I finally faced it and got closer, I was able to barely discern the shape of my brother's body. It was a shock when I first saw him; I cried out in a grief-stricken wail. Was he alive? Was he dead? Did he suffer? Was there something I could or should do to move him? I could not conceive of any way to move him since I could barely move myself. But one thing was very clear. Like me, he was no longer in his seat. I inched forward to get as close to my brother as possible. From my closest position I could barely reach out far enough to touch his exposed left ankle above his work boot with my outstretched right hand. When I touched him, I could not tell if he felt cold because I was so cold, but I definitely felt no body heat. He was inert and motionless—so still, that after several minutes, while stretched out touching his upper ankle—I knew he had to be dead.

There was something odd about the picture, though. His body seemed to be resting in a location far to the rear of where his seat was located in the plane wreckage. Yet I had been catapulted forward and had found myself well in front of the airplane wreckage. Then I remembered my mental, slow-motion, reenacting image of the last second of our flight, and I realized it coincided with both where I found myself, and what I was looking at now. This realization further reinforced my belief that what had been replaying in my mind really was a detailed mental recording of the last second of my flight. I pondered whether some obstruction—possibly a tree, or perhaps even the top of the aircraft cabin, as it was peeled back like a sardine can lid, had caught my brother and lifted him from his seat as the plane moved forward in the last few feet of its earth-bound trajectory. A few milliseconds later, I was launched forward by my own momentum as the airplane's forward motion came to an almost instantaneous halt when it hit the ground. Simultaneously, I was carried upward by the thrust of the collapsing cabin floor as the plane pancaked onto the ground. I was thrown upward and over the aircraft instrument panel with incredible force. Soon I would come to understand that my leg injuries indicated I had actually collided with the instrument panel as I was ejected from the plane by the force of the crash. I seemed to have an inner compulsion to put all the puzzle pieces together into a coherent pattern that made some kind of sense.

A newspaper photo. (photo used by permission from *The Northern Virginia Daily,* Strasburg, VA)

The airplane fuselage was lying on its left side and the entire cabin roof was gone along with the wings, both cabin doors, and the surrounding structures. Both front seats were completely exposed but still firmly attached to the cabin floor with the right seat above the left seat because the fuselage was on its left side. The pilot's seat was positioned exactly at ground level. With painful effort, I rotated myself from my downward-facing prone position to facing upward on my back. Again, I hooked my right foot under my left ankle to force my left lower leg to rotate with the rest of me but I grunted with pain in a non-human, low, bestial tone as I made the transition. Once I recovered a bit and was facing skyward, I pushed myself up into a sitting position and then backward toward the left pilot's seat, using my arms while dragging my legs until my back rested against the pilot's seat bottom cushion. The same strange and inhuman sounds seemed to come from somewhere deep inside me as I forced myself back to the seat. This was where I stayed for the remainder of the time I was on the mountain. I threw the fleece-lined jacket I had found over my freezing feet. But they never did feel any warmer and burned with cold, if that makes sense.

Once I was sitting and relatively still, I began to drift into and out of consciousness again. Whether I was falling into true unconsciousness or simply falling asleep, I do not really know. But I do remember that I wished I could remain unconscious or at least oblivious. Regardless of what I wished for, the cold rain that soaked me, kept reviving me from sleep or unconsciousness. When I would wake up, I would be moaning. At one time, in a fit of self-pity, grief, and guilt, I wished for my own death. But I then felt utterly ashamed to be thinking such self-centered thoughts. I realized death might end my own physical and emotional suffering but it would result in additional pain and suffering for my wife and family. And there was also my unborn child to consider. During my unconscious times there was the dream—always the dream.

Sometime during the night, during a period of consciousness, in an effort to tactilely explore the area immediately around me, I reached out to my left as far as my arm could extend into the blackness of the area behind the pilot's seat. I had already crawled across hundreds of crumpled pages from the Jeppesen approach plate loose-leaf binder that had burst open. The pages littered the area all around me along with other small and diverse pieces of wreckage. To my amazement, when I reached out, my hand fell directly on an object I instantly recognized as the plane's ELT, the emergency locator transmitter. The FAA had only begun requiring all private aircraft to be equipped with an ELT in 1973, and small aircraft ELT technology was in its relative infancy. This ELT unit had been mounted on the rear cabin wall directly behind the pilot's seat. The rear cabin wall had disappeared, but somehow, the ELT had not disappeared with it and had fallen where my hand could find it as I blindly probed from my stationary sitting position.

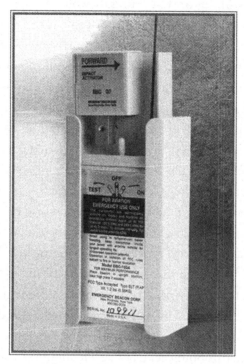

The ELT radio transmitter model
mounted in my aircraft.

The ELT was a small battery powered transmitter that was designed to transmit a distress signal on 121.5 megahertz, the universal aviation emergency-use-only frequency. It was supposed to be triggered by the G forces of a crash and automatically begin transmitting. Commercial aircraft in flight were supposed to monitor this frequency and all air traffic control facilities continually monitored this frequency. Today, satellites automatically and continuously monitor this frequency everywhere around the world, but this satellite monitoring system did not exist at the time of my accident.

When I moved the ELT directly in front of my face, inches from my squinting left eye, and began to explore it with my fingers, I realized the trigger mechanism was jammed in the OFF position instead of the ON position. I was able to bend a deformed and interfering aluminum tab clear of the switch so I could manually switch it ON. I did not know if the radio was working or if any aircraft would pick up the signal or if I was close enough to any FAA control facility, but it gave me a small measure of hope. I had heard jet aircraft overflying the area throughout the night and into the next day. (As it turns out, no aircraft or control facility ever acknowledged picking up the distress signal.)

As the hours passed, I was never so miserably cold in my entire life. I shivered convulsively in great, wracking, tremulous waves throughout the night and the next day. My feet and toes ached with cold. I did not know the full extent of my injuries except for my obviously fractured left femur and the facial/eye injury that refused to stop bleeding. The entire time I was on the mountain I felt fresh warm blood oozing from the wound involving my right eye and dripping down my face. I could not possibly imagine what I looked like. I was also enveloped by a deep bass-note throbbing ache that seemed to engulf my entire lower body. My lower back throbbed and ached, both legs ached and my feet ached from the cold. But it was my pelvis that seemed to especially ache in a way that couldn't be relieved by shifting my weight in any manner. I remembered the throbbing ache I once felt about six years before due to a broken ankle. So the continual throbbing ache I now felt throughout my lower body made me suspect I had more fractures than just a broken left leg.

Later I learned, in addition to my fractured left femur, I had three fractured lumbar vertebrae, a fractured sacrum, a dislocated or fractured coccyx, two fractures of my pelvis, and a fractured right tibia and right patella. My right ankle was severely sprained and it was later suspected it also had been fractured. I had also done irreversible and significant damage to several discs between vertebrae. I was bleeding, both internally due to the fractured pelvis, and externally from multiple lacerations and cuts all over my scalp, face, and limbs—the worst of which seemed to be over my right eye. That wound also severed a major nerve servicing the front right quadrant of my scalp, leaving me with permanent numbness in that area. (Yes, I really am a numbskull in case you already suspected it.) I would also eventually learn I had another significant wound that would remain overlooked and undiscovered by the medical staff in two hospitals until almost two weeks into my hospitalization.

The view looking south from crash site
toward the direction of approach.

Eventually, the first diffused light of dawn began to creep over the area, and I could see a bit more from my left eye. Due to the general swelling of my face, however, opening my left eye was difficult and only intermittently possible with concerted effort. What vision I had was extremely limited. At times, I had to pry my left eye open and hold it open with my fingers in order to see. The black shapes became more defined but my environment was enshrouded in heavy fog. I could not see more than 50 feet in any direction. The hard cold rain had continued all during the night, but it was easing up into a sustained but moderate drizzle as dawn broke. The temperature still continued to drop and, being soaked by the rain, I gradually realized I was in danger of succumbing to hypothermia.

Mark's body, lying about four feet to my left, revealed itself in greater detail as the morning light strengthened. He was positioned face-down and seemed to be jackknifed over some part of the wreckage. His legs were outstretched and the toes of his work boots were the only part of his body that actually touched the ground. He was wedged next to a tree that was still standing among the wreckage. He was draped over something that kept his upper body suspended high enough to allow his arms to hang straight down from his shoulders without his hands touching the ground. His head was fully pitched forward between his dangling arms. Mark's arms partially obstructed my view of his face. Nevertheless, I could see enough to know he had bled profusely from a head wound that seemed to be located in the same general area as my own bleeding wound. I wondered if we were both hit by the same object but Mark had taken a more direct and fatal blow.

All during the night and continuing into the daylight hours of Wednesday, as I lay near his body, whenever I was conscious I thought about the heartache my parents would know as a result of my failure as a pilot. I remained conscious from daybreak onward and I wondered how they would get the news. As the pilot of an aircraft I had committed the worst offense possible; I had somehow caused the death of another who had placed his trust in me as the pilot. And yet I also thought about the reality of where my brother was at that very moment. I realized, totally by the grace of God, Mark was joyfully standing in the presence of Jesus as he had trusted Christ for salvation about five years before. The change in his life had been dramatic and was evidence that Christ and the power of the Gospel through the Holy Spirit, had taken hold of him and changed him into a different person. Only that knowledge, and the truth of the promises contained in scripture on which I had based my own life, gave me assurance and kept me from descending into a totally black abyss of despair as I contemplated his body lying next to me the entire time I was sitting on the ground with my back supported by the pilot's seat cushion. Even so, I had some desperate conversations with God.

As the pain and cold took hold of me with its unyielding iron grip, I said some ridiculous things to God and I said them out loud as if I was trying to draw God's attention to myself. "Is this what you call—rising up on the wings of eagles?" I mumbled. "Is this what you call--not letting me dash my foot against a stone?" I was actually, with intention, throwing God's own scripture back into his face—not to mention ripping it out of context as I quoted these passages from Isaiah and the Psalms with the sharp edge of sarcasm and bitterness in my voice. But as these words came into my mind and out of my mouth, I had a mental image of myself in the very presence of Jesus, and I felt ashamed for what I thought and said even as I said it. I saw Christ standing next to me, comforting me. I could see him as He smiled and shook his head in understanding and sympathy at my foolishness, just as a wise and tolerant earthly father would patiently endure the foolishness of a young son who couldn't help himself. Words came to me with such clarity; it almost seemed as if they were spoken audibly. It seemed He said directly to me, *"I know. I know. I know how you feel, and I understand. And I know where you are, even if you don't. Don't give up."*

The question of where I was also occupied my mind throughout the night. I knew I wasn't very far in terms of miles from the Linden VOR. But I didn't know how far I was from any actual civilization. I'd heard absolutely nothing during the night to indicate I was near any human habitation or road of any kind. There were absolutely no sounds, no bird chirps, no animals moving over the leaf-covered ground, and certainly no traffic noise. There was only the sound of rain falling through the trees and the occasional jet planes passing overhead. I assumed these planes were flying into and out of Washington because they were loud enough to be below normal jet cruising altitudes. I also knew I was probably on top of a mountain. I had known I was flying into rising terrain, but I never expected it to be higher than 3000 feet MSL in the area of my flight. Because I was so occupied with my brother, my family, thinking about my decision process that led to this situation, and dealing with my immediate cold and pain, I didn't actually spend much time pondering my future and my own ultimate fate. At one point I fantastically imagined I should hoist myself onto my feet and try to walk. Where I would go I did not know, but I foolishly thought I could strap the tow bar to my left leg using my belt, find a downed limb to use as a crutch, and hobble away. I actually said to myself, *just let me rest for a little while longer and then I'll try to get up and get out of here*. I said this to myself several times during the night, but I'd put off the attempt by telling myself I just needed to rest a bit longer to regain my strength. The trouble was I was losing strength with every passing minute as blood loss and hypothermia were taking their toll.

I wasn't sure anybody at home would even consider us missing because of my open-ended plans. They may have thought we were on our way to Waxhaw NC to visit friends. I didn't think anyone at home would become really worried unless they hadn't heard from us by sometime on Wednesday. How long would it take for them to realize things had gone wrong? The FAA wouldn't be looking because I had flown without filing a flight plan. This was totally legal when flying VFR cross country even if, in hindsight, it was another foolish thing to do.

Daybreak advanced to the full light of day but it remained darkly gloomy, gray, damp, and freezing during the ensuing daylight hours. In fact I was told later the temperature dropped right to the freezing point, 32 Deg. F. My convulsive palsy-like violent shivering continued unabated. It seemed as if I was being shaken in different directions by multiple giant hands. My shaking was totally uncontrollable. I could not make myself stop with any amount of concentration.

I did make one interesting discovery as the daylight hours passed; I found my missing right shoe only inches from where I sat. It was literally embedded in the face of the instrument panel next to my head as I sat there but I didn't see it until it was completely light. It took all my strength and more than a few attempts for me to pry it out of the panel, a testament to the force of the impact between my foot and the instrument panel. I speculated; when the airplane met the ground and the ground crushed the belly of the plane and launched me upward, my right leg rose higher than my left. I still can't fathom how my legs even got out from beneath the instrument panel as I was propelled upward and forward. My feet would have been resting on the rudder pedals well beneath the instrument panel at the moment of the crash. My right foot had smashed against the instrument panel, imbedding itself as I was propelled forward, while my left leg caught the top of the instrument panel, just above my knee, fracturing the strongest bone in my body. I could see the crushed top edge of the panel exactly as it was impressed by my leg.

A crash site photo taken in April from the
same spot as newspaper photo.

As time passed, I fully comprehended and accepted as fact that hypothermia was the real enemy and, given enough time, it would kill me. Later in the day, as my energy level sunk to its lowest level, I really felt the specter of death hanging over me. It was almost a palpable presence that I really can't find words to describe but, amazingly, I never totally lost hope. I told myself God would not take my brother in an instant—at least I hoped he had died in an instant—and then allow me to painfully linger, finally to the point of death. It did not make sense to me. If I was destined to die on this mountain, I reasoned, why wouldn't God take me at the same time my brother entered his presence? What could be the point of this suffering? I wonder how God felt about my simplistic and self-serving logic.

Much later on in my recovery, I really began to appreciate the fact that God had created the perfect meat-locker conditions to keep me alive for the fifteen or sixteen hours I was on the mountain—conditions meant to keep me alive just long enough and no longer. Under more benign and temperate conditions, complications resulting from deepening shock would have rapidly escalated to fatal levels. But the ice bath God created chilled me to the marrow and lowered my core body temperature enough to retard and delay this inevitability. At the same time, it was not quite so cold that I would die from hypothermia within the time-frame of my exposure. Not only had God miraculously spared me from death due to the blunt-force trauma of a high-speed crash directly into a mountaintop, but post-crash, He kept me delicately balanced on the knife-edge that separated life and death. And though the conditions were absolutely miserable, I now think they actually kept me alive.

I never really knew the time because of my missing wrist watch, but I sensed we were moving into the afternoon hours and I could feel the strength continuing to drain from my body. I no longer fantasized about walking away as I barely had the strength to hold my head up. I knew this could not continue much longer and my future life-span was going to be measured in, at most, a few hours and certainly not in days. I fully accepted the truth that I would not survive another night. This is when I audibly uttered my last prayer, if you can even call it a prayer. But I was directly addressing my Lord with my words. I said out loud, "Lord, if you don't get me off this mountain in the next hour, I'm going to be talking to you face-to-face." I don't know if I meant this as a threat or as an expression of my submission to his will, but those were my exact words to him.

CHAPTER 6

RESCUED

I let some time pass. After all, I had magnanimously given God another hour to meet His most pressing request. At most, I think I waited the hour I had given God. Then something inside me said now was the time. I was completely out of strength and, one way or another, God was going to remove me from this mountain torment—either directly into His presence or by means of some kind of earthly salvation of human origin. At that moment—for only the second time since arriving in this silent foggy world—I called out for help as if someone was near enough to hear me. I called out twice with what energy I had left…

Then, to my complete astonishment and amazement, there was a voice. A voice in the distance answered me.

For the very first time, I could hear distant footsteps in the leaves instead of total silence. The footsteps started to approach at a quickening pace. The voice called out to me, "Where are you?" I weakly answered, "Over here!" The voice called out again and again I answered with what strength I had. The footsteps came closer and a young man appeared out of the fog and stood over me. He was dressed in a quilted jacket and equipped with a backpack and trekking poles. Even with my compromised vision I could tell his eyes were darting here and there as he surveyed the scene before him, trying to take it in and make sense of it. He looked me over and audibly gasped, swearing several times in the process. His head jerked side-to-side, his gaze quickly moving from one detail to another as he stood over me, backing up once or twice in the process. I actually smiled imagining my own reaction if, while walking through the woods and minding my own business, I suddenly encountered a crumpled airplane, a dead body, and a bloody and battered survivor. My reaction might have been similar to his but, since the tables were turned, I just told him he was the most direct answer to prayer I'd ever received. He seemed confused and at a total loss and only managed to stammer out a question asking what I wanted him to do. I immediately told him he had to go get help. He ignored my earlier comment about answered prayer and expressed questioning surprise that I wanted him to leave me after he had just found me. I repeated that he had to go and get help, but I added a request for something to drink if he had anything with him. My mouth was parched and my tongue was swelling. He immediately took off his backpack and pulled out two small juice boxes, inserted the straws and gave them to me. I drank the most delicious orange juice I have ever tasted.

I then asked my rescuer for his name. He answered, giving me his name. It was Jim. I continued with my questions and asked him where I was, even as I realized I was preventing him from leaving to get help—the very thing I first told him he had to do for me. He told me I was in the Shenandoah National Park just off the Appalachian Trail and he found me because he was hiking the trail. I followed up and asked him how far he had to go for help. He explained I was only about a quarter mile up the trail from where it crossed Skyline Drive at mile-marker sixteen but I was, perhaps, a few hundred feet higher than Skyline Drive as the south-bound trail ascends from there and runs along the crest of the mountain ridge. He said he'd have to go down to Skyline Drive and wait for a passing car. (No cell phones existed then.) The trouble was, since the weather was so bad and the fog was so thick, he had no idea how long it would take for a car to even appear. He said he just hoped the park rangers had not already closed Skyline Drive to transient traffic because of the fog. He continued to explain that once he flagged a car, the car would have to drive about twelve miles to the ranger station near the north entrance of the park. Then the rangers would have to summon an ambulance crew from Front Royal which was at least twenty driving miles from our location. I told him in that case, he'd better leave now, but I also asked him if he was carrying any extra clothing I could put on while he was away. He immediately took off his own down-filled jacket and put it on me. His body heat still lingered in the down filling as he put it on me. It felt indescribably wonderful and I knew, no matter how long it took, I was going to will myself to survive, no matter what. I thanked him over and over, and he finally took his leave to go get help.

It seemed like Jim was gone for at least an hour during which time I was left to my own thoughts, but eventually he returned and reported he had succeeded in stopping a passing car. He said the driver promised to carry the message to the nearest ranger station that an airplane crash had occurred in their park and there was a survivor who needed immediate help.

As we waited for help to arrive, I asked my personal "trail-angel" a question that had puzzled me the entire time he was gone—what was he doing out hiking on a day like today? (For Appalachian Trail hikers, the term *trail angel* has a specific meaning—someone who leaves or supplies food and/or other aid to assist through-hikers on their journey.)

Jim then offered me a lengthy explanation for his presence at that moment in this place. He told me he lived and worked in Washington, DC; he was dealing with some kind of personal problem and had decided to take the day off. Despite the bad weather, he'd decided to go on a hike in order to get away and think things over. He told me hiking was his favorite outdoor wilderness activity, and with obvious pride, he revealed he was a "2000-miler." He had section-hiked the entire 2,168 mile length of the Appalachian Trail from Maine to Georgia. He said he did it in large sections as he had vacation time to devote to it. He was accustomed to hiking in bad weather because, as he explained, if you schedule a multi-day wilderness-trail hike, you must continue on no matter what kind of weather you walk into.

Pilot Rescued After Crash; Brother Killed

Front Royal rescue squadsmen and Shenandoah National Park officials Tuesday afternoon rescued the pilot of a single-engine plane that crashed on the summit of Mount South Marshall Tuesday night, killing the pilot's brother.

Dan Lipsi, 30, of Perkasie, Pa., who survived a night of freezing temperatures strapped to the pilot's seat of the Cessna aircraft was treated initially at Warren Memorial Hospital Wednesday and transferred to Winchester Memorial Hospital.

His brother, Mark, 27, was pronounced dead at the scene of the crash, about 100 feet off the Appalachian Trail and about one-quarter of a mile from Milepost 16 on the Skyline Drive.

The remains of the plane, which disintegrated on impact into dozens of pieces, was discovered by a hiker on the trail around 1 p.m., Wednesday. He notified park officials in Front Royal who descended on the fog-swept mountains, with an elevation of 3,212 feet.

A park official said the pilot told him the crash occurred around 10 p.m. and that the brothers were on their way home from Raleigh, N.C.

The plane sheared off the top of the uppermost trees on the east face of the summit and it appeared would have cleared the top with another 20 feet of elevation. The exposed cockpit of the plane came to rest approximately 200 feet from the point where it first struck tree limbs.

Wednesday's crash occurred within one mile of a plane crash which killed two men in November 1975. Four persons died in a third crash in the same vicinity in October 1968.

The Federal Aviation Administration was investigating the accident.

Jet Fighters Buzz Beirut

BEIRUT, Lebanon (AP) — Low-flying jet fighters buzzed Beirut Thursday, drawing anti-aircraft fire from Palestinian guerrillas and Syrian peacekeeping forces.

The rightist Voice of Lebanon radio claimed they were Israeli, but the military command in Tel Aviv denied Israeli planes flew over Beirut. "There is no truth to this report," a spokesman said.

Witnesses saw a pair of warplanes swoop in from the sea just above rooftop level.

Daily Staff Photo

Survivor Of Plane Crash In Warren

Front Royal Rescue Squad members and Shenandoah National Park personnel carry out Dan Lipsi, 30, of Perkasie, Pa., who was critically injured when the Cessna single-engine plane he was piloting crashed near the summit of 3,212-foot Mount South Marshall Tuesday night. His brother, Mark, 27, was killed in the crash.

(Photo used by permission from *The Northern Virginia Daily*, Strasburg, VA.)

As he spoke, it dawned on me that God had put the wheels in motion for him to be there at the exact moment I called out for help. Because of the fog, he had to be near enough to hear my feeble cry for help or it's possible he would have passed by without notice since the crash site was off the trail and screened by trees and fog, and hikers are usually concentrating on their feet to avoid tripping over various obstacles in their path. This was especially true in conditions where there was little or no scenery to view because of poor visibility. God had worked things out in His perfect timing long before, maybe days or even weeks before I uttered my last prayer to Him. Jim was a living, walking miracle of God's timing and it reflected His grace and love toward me and my family. I simply told Jim again that he was an answer to prayer, but he never showed any sign of acknowledging it or even hearing me. I have no idea what he was thinking. Those statements from me seemed to make no impression on him.

I asked Jim what time it was. He said it was around one p.m. It took at least another hour for help to arrive. First the rangers arrived and, eventually, an EMT/rescue crew. From the time Jim found me until the time the EMT crew arrived, two to three hours had passed. When the EMT crew arrived there were at least four men and two park rangers, plus Jim. A couple of the EMTs attended to me, one spent time interviewing Jim and the other just looked over the situation waiting for orders from the man in charge.

The ranger who seemed to be in charge asked me a hundred questions about my condition and also what I thought had led to the crash. In my weakened state, I mumbled out answers and unguardedly speculated on the cause of the crash—openly confessing it was all my fault. I never realized that his questions and my answers would be recorded in an affidavit that would eventually become part of the evidence file collected by the NTSB (National Transportation Safety Board) as part of their accident investigation.

The crew prepared me to be moved assuming I might have a broken back. They splinted both of my legs and my neck. They swaddled my head between two large rectangular foam blocks. Then they gently placed a back board beneath me. The EMTs had removed Jim's jacket when they first started to work on me, so I know he got it back. But I'm not sure what shape it was in since, as far as I could tell, I was pretty much covered in blood, especially around my face and neck. After I was secured to the back-board, I was strapped into a metal basket- stretcher and then hand-carried down the Appalachian Trail the quarter mile to the waiting ambulance.

Since my total attention was taken up by the men working on me, I wasn't sure if Jim was still on the scene when I was taken away. But the reality was, I was gone without a goodbye passing between us. During the ambulance ride as I thought about it, it seemed as if Jim had vanished into the fog just as suddenly as he had appeared. I never saw or spoke to him again although there is some circumstantial evidence indicating my father may have spoken to him in the days following the accident.

I was put onto a gurney in the ambulance and driven to a small county hospital near Front Royal, Virginia. As we drove, I began to drift off, but I was not positioned very well on the gurney and was very uncomfortable; my head was off the end and unsupported. I had to hold it up with one arm tucked behind it. Even at this early point, I began to privately question my medical treatment. I thought it strange that the EMTs were so careful to place my head between two large foam blocks to stabilize my neck, yet the ambulance crew seemed unconcerned that I had to support it with one arm during the ambulance trip. Even after I complained about this to the attendant sitting next to me, he did absolutely nothing to alleviate the problem during the ride. As I endured the trip in the semidarkness of the ambulance's interior, it seemed eerie to hear the ambulance siren wailing from inside the ambulance instead of outside. I'd never been in an ambulance before as a patient, and it was strange to realize the siren I heard was for my benefit and not meant for somebody else.

CHAPTER 7

VIRGINIA HOSPITALS

*M*y arrival at the county hospital signaled the start of a whirlwind of activity by the medical staff on my behalf. My clothes were all unceremoniously cut off—no fiddling with buttons, zippers, trouser legs, or sleeves. The worst of the blood and filth was cleaned off my body as best they could, but it was not a complete job by any means. A full body x-ray panel was performed after which some of my wounds were further cleaned and some were sutured. A very compassionate and folksy ophthalmic surgeon arrived to treat the wound near my right eye. He expertly and delicately sutured the wound around the orbit of my right eye while keeping up a quaint and homey monologue as he worked away. It took over thirty stitches to close that wound. He was fearful I had ruptured the eye because one-hundred percent of what should have been white was blood red. That proved not to be the case. However, I would have double vision when I was eventually able to open my right eye. The surgeon said this was due to the extreme swelling of the tissues around my eye which restricted the movement of the muscles controlling it. This condition lasted for the next four or five weeks after which my vision returned to normal. Because of the double vision, I have little visual memory of the weeks I spent in any of the Virginia hospitals or of the first weeks after I was transferred to a Pennsylvania hospital.

While in the emergency room at this county hospital, I was also able to speak to my family by phone. My first conversation with my father was very difficult. At the time, I had no idea how much my family knew about what had taken place. How could I possibly apologize to him for the death of my brother—his second-born son? Unbeknownst to me, however, the local police had already spoken to my father and he knew my brother was gone. My father was very compassionate as we spoke. Even as I knew he was working through his own grief, I realized he was trying to comfort me in mine. I also spoke to my dear wife and did my best to reassure her. Speaking was difficult because my face and lips were so swollen and it was difficult to make myself understood, but I assured her I was going to be okay, even if I did not really know this to be true with complete certainty.

Eventually, an orthopedist came to speak to me and described the various fractures I had incurred as revealed by the x-ray panel. After running down the list of fractures, he told me this small county hospital was not adequately equipped to handle me on a long term basis, and he was only a sole practitioner and could not provide the kind of attention and follow-up I needed. He said it would be best if I were transferred to a larger hospital in Winchester where there were better facilities plus an orthopedic practice consisting of multiple doctors. I was certainly in no position to argue with him so I gave my approval for the plan and was prepped for a second ambulance trip heading for Winchester, Virginia. I said my goodbyes to the hospital staff and thanked them for being there for me. Then we drove off to Winchester.

It was well after dark and into the night by the time we left this hospital near Front Royal. Thankfully, the ride to Winchester was more comfortable than my ambulance ride coming off the mountain since it was a considerably longer ride. I probably dozed on and off during the trip, but I do remember the interior lights being dimmed to a soft glow and the ambulance EMT worker sitting next to me, who tried to make me as comfortable as he could. I felt better simply because I was starting to warm up, except for my feet that continued to throb with cold. Also, I desperately wanted something to drink. However, that was one thing no one would provide for me for reasons that I didn't fully understand at the time. My mouth was desert dry and my tongue felt like it was twice its normal size.

Arriving at the hospital in Winchester, there was a repeat of the whirlwind activity by the ER staff, all centered on—me. I felt sorry for the other ER patients already in curtained cubicles in the ER when I arrived. They were forced to wait as everyone on the ER staff seemed to be involved with the emergency case that just arrived. I remember one unlucky fellow who was holding a bandaged hand vociferously complaining he was still in pain and he wanted something for it. A nurse apologized to him and explained he would just have to be patient as they were doing their best. I couldn't see him very well through my squinting left eye, but I detected a very annoyed expression on his face that matched the annoyance in his voice.

Very soon after my arrival, I met the orthopedic surgeon who was assigned to handle my case while I was in Winchester. He was younger than the orthopedic surgeon who first saw me at Front Royal. He introduced himself and volunteered the information that he had a tour in Vietnam and was experienced in putting broken bodies back together after violent trauma. I guess he was trying to reassure me. I'm not sure why but, from the very start, we seemed to get along quite well. Over the next couple of weeks, he seemed to show more interest in me than just another orthopedic case. There were times when he came into my hospital room just to sit and chat with Donna and me. To this day he remains the one and only hospital doctor, among many I have dealt with over the years, to do this. He seemed to actually enjoy the time spent with us. My new doctor discussed his recommended plan of treatment. I was to be placed in skeletal traction and would eventually be fitted with something he called a cast-brace before I was well enough to be shipped home.

While still in the ER, I was transferred to the hospital bed I would occupy until I left Winchester. Using a hand-cranked brace and bit, my surgeon began the traction procedure by drilling directly through my skin and through my shin bone below the left knee. Then a stainless steel all-thread rod was threaded into and through my shin bone. The rod emerged from the opposite side of the bone, protruding on both the entrance and exit sides. This rod would provide an attachment point for the traction weights.

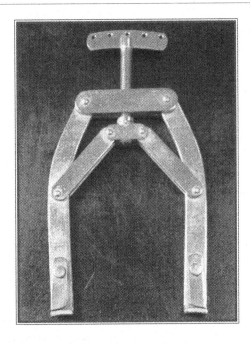

A shiny chrome horseshoe-shaped clamp mechanism (I still have it) was clamped to the ends of the rod that had just been inserted into my shin bone, and a cord was tied to the clamp. The cord was then routed over a pulley at the end of the bed, and attached to 40-plus pounds of traction weights.

Before the weights were hung, two nurses draped themselves across my chest, one on each side of my bed, and held me down. Where did they think I was going to go? But I was told this was necessary to keep me from sliding down the bed while the weights were hung. Or maybe, as was suggested by some wag in the room, they just liked me! (Not likely, and certainly not that much!) The face of the closest nurse was only inches from my own. Her chest and that of the other nurse pressed down against my own torso as they firmly grasped opposite sides of the mattress, using their combined body-weight to pin me down. I remember one nurse was very pleasant and spoke with a fetching Australian accent as I had chatted with her during much of my workup. I cannot remember her name, so I will call her Sally. Because of the absurdity of what I was experiencing, I said, "Sally…" She turned her head and looked directly at me as I dead-panned, "You know we can't go on meeting like this!" The entire medical staff in the room broke out in laughter. My surgeon completely stopped what he was doing and just laughed for a few seconds. Later, he told me he knew I was going to make it based on this minor attempt at humor under the circumstances. As the weights were hung, it felt like my left leg stretched at least six inches, but I'm sure it was less. It was a surreal experience. Then an aluminum framed hammock-like support was placed under my leg and more ropes, pulleys and weights were added to the mix. My leg was then cradled in the hammock support which was, itself, floating off the bed surface because of the attached ropes and counterweights. And while all this was happening, whenever they had a chance, other nurses were cleaning my various cuts and lacerations, and bathing me as much as possible. Yet despite their attention to detail, everyone in two different hospitals missed a significant wound located at the base of my spine. I suppose it was because I was flat on my back. They also omitted washing my hands, which were still caked with grime and blood. When it looked like the nurses were finished, I asked them if they could please wash my hands too. They apologized for the oversight and thoroughly washed them. In addition to all the orthopedic work, I was catheterized (oh, joy!) and multiple IV lines were started anywhere they could find a place to insert one—or so it seemed to me. Eventually I was ready for the ride to ICU. By this time it was sometime between eleven p.m. and midnight, Wednesday night. Soon it would be Thanksgiving Day. I wondered what was going on at home.

The ICU was a very large multiple bed facility typical of a major city hospital. Here I experienced another example of God's grace. Instead of being placed in one of the beds in the common ward, I was placed in an isolated room that was partitioned off the main ICU floor by window-filled office partitions that did not extend as high as the ceiling, but provided a fair amount of seclusion from the rest of the floor. This was the only bed in the ICU with this benefit. The hustle and bustle of the ICU unit never stopped, day or night. The fact that I was in a semi-isolated room allowed me the luxury of some measure of peace and quiet during the nights I was there. The room actually was a haven for some of the staff while I was there. Many came in to just chat when they had a break. Some said they enjoyed the classical music I listened to on a radio that was lent to me by the ICU nursing staff. One night, a young but exhausted nurse came in and sat down in the chair next to my bed. I asked what was bothering her because her head was in her hands. She looked up and told me it was an unusually hard day. She said five people had died on the floor that day on her shift. She said it was nice to spend some time with someone she knew was going to get well.

I have never met better people than those who worked in the ICU. They were kind, compassionate, attentive, and intelligent.

I was attached to a variety of monitors, oxygen, and IV drips adding to the rat's nest of tubes already attached to me. I noted in particular that I was being transfused with whole blood. In total, I was administered five units of blood. I had lost almost half my total blood supply due to both internal and external bleeding. Finally, I seemed to be fully *assembled* and things quieted down. I became aware of a quiet but steady *beep...beep...beep* from a monitor confirming that I was still among the land of the living.

At this time, there was only one nurse still by my side. She was busy adjusting IV drips. I asked her if I could finally have something to alleviate my pain. As she continued to inspect the IV drips with her back half turned away from me, she casually asked, "...well—when was the last time they gave you anything?" I answered, "I'm pretty sure I haven't gotten anything yet." She spun around, giving me a very doubtful look then picked up my chart and rifled through it. She looked up and said, "I can't believe it, but it looks like you're right!" Apparently, I was uncharacteristically calm and uncomplaining (totally God's grace and peace) up until now compared with many other multiple trauma patients. Or maybe I was just numb from the cold; it took me days before I felt really warm—especially my feet that had experienced a touch of frostbite. But because I was not screaming for pain relief, no one had offered me any, even during the traction procedure. The nurse literally ran out the room and in thirty seconds came back with an injection of Demerol. Finally—blessed relief and sleep—if only for an hour or two. For the next two weeks Demerol would become my best friend, next to my attentive and loving wife.

My youngest brother, Pete, and my dear wife, Donna, left home for the drive to Winchester as soon as they could organize the trip on Wednesday evening. They drove straight through and arrived around three a.m. on Thanksgiving Day. The ICU staff briefed Donna and Pete regarding what they were going to see and reassured them that the mass of tubes, wires, monitors, and machines forming the cocoon around me did not mean my life was hanging in the balance. Donna approached me, and even with only one eye partially open, I could tell she was dismayed at the sight that confronted her. Nevertheless, she bravely planted a kiss on my excessively swollen, blood-caked and cracked lips, trying to ignore the multicolored marshmallow my face had become behind the ballooned lips she had just favored with her kiss.

Shortly after they arrived at the ICU, Donna asked if there was anything she could eat because she was three months pregnant, had not eaten for many hours, and was feeling nauseous. The gracious ICU staff scurried around to round up some of their own food—some left over birthday cake and one packaged deli sandwich, all they had at that time of the morning. They never failed to show compassion and kindness the entire time I was with them.

Donna and Pete soon left me after their short visit to continue their drive down to Front Royal where Pete was required to identify the body of his brother. They then drove back to Winchester to their motel to get a few hours of sleep after their exhausting ordeal.

After Donna and Pete left me, but before any other family members had arrived, an NTSB investigator appeared at my bedside in the ICU. It was still early on Thanksgiving morning. Today, I can only suppose that, once he flashed his federal ID badge, the nursing staff felt compelled to admit him. I do know I was under the influence of Demerol and I just wanted to sleep but the investigator came for a statement, and apparently, he wasn't leaving without one. He proceeded to ask his questions and I drowsily stumbled out my answers. Earlier, I had already miss-stated to Donna that I had crashed in North Carolina, an indication that I wasn't thinking too clearly and I had similar trouble with the NTSB examiner. I incorrectly stated to him that the date of the accident was the twenty-second, an indication of the addled state of my brain at the time he questioned me. Nevertheless, this misinformation was dutifully recorded by my questioner and became part of my statement. The investigator wrote down my responses to his questions. Then he composed a narrative text that was, more-or-less, in my own words. I was required to sign the summary statement after he read it back to me. This statement became part of the accident investigation record as did my earlier statements given to the park ranger who first questioned me while I was still on the mountain. I would see both of these documents again later. In hindsight, even if they had a job to do, I think this action by the NTSB was unfair and intrusive. Adding insult to injury, not long after while still in the ICU and while dealing with similar cognitive limitations, I was asked to provide statements to the aircraft insurance company. Again, I had no control over the timing of the interview and I did not have the presence of mind to refuse it. The insurance rep's intrusion annoyed me even more than the NTSB's. I now wish I had had an advocate or I had sufficient wits about me to tell them both to take a hike until I felt stronger and more lucid.

In addition to Donna and Pete, my pastor and other family members traveled down to Winchester to see me later on Thanksgiving Day. I was visited then by my parents, an uncle and aunt who were in the States from Brazil, and my youngest sister, Janet. A day or two later, my older sister, Nancy, and her husband arrived after they drove up directly from Florida, leaving early from their vacation. Marion and her husband, Rick, also came down later. Marion was initially tasked with staying at my parent's house in their absence over the Thanksgiving holidays to handle the many telephone calls that came to the house in the days immediately following the accident. It was lonely work for her as the rest of my family was with me.

The NTSB accident investigation team completed their on-site investigation by the end of Thanksgiving Day after which the park rangers said they wanted the wreckage removed as quickly as possible since it was just off the Appalachian Trail in a National Park. Pete was called upon to complete this task. He would be required to remove the wreckage of the airplane, a wheel barrow load at a time, chopping it apart into manageable pieces using an ax, hacksaw, wire cutters, and a bolt cutter. Some sympathetic pilots from the Front Royal airport lent him the tools and the airport manager lent him a stake-body truck to transport the wreckage to the nearest scrap yard.

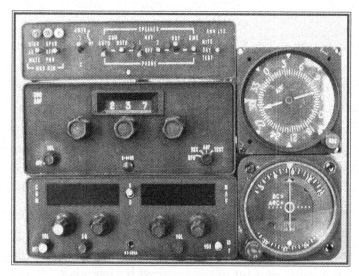

Some salvaged radios and instruments.

What a back-breaking job this was for Pete. Toward the end of this task, a brother-in-law and even my youngest sister were present on the scene and they were able to offer Pete a helping hand. But it was exhausting and ghoulish work for him and he completed the vast majority of this task by himself in lonely solitude. I think the demands of this task caused Pete to experience Mark's loss in an intensely personal way that was different from either me or my other siblings. It probably felt like a true burial to Pete as he carried each piece of the wreckage off the mountain ultimately to dispose of it at a local scrap yard. And although he may not have realized it at that very moment, losing Mark would also ultimately result in the loss of Pete's own career dreams.

Pete was a skilled wood worker and craftsman with an artistic bent. This was the career path he had chosen for himself and the path he had been pursuing before the accident. But with the loss of Mark, he felt he was needed in the family business. He left his job and his previous employer to work in the family business and he applied himself to this new reality with the same intensity as he approached the work he loved and had chosen for himself. He may never admit that he selflessly sacrificed his personal aspirations to work in the family business, but over the years, we came to appreciate what a sacrifice he made. Thank you, Pete.

Also, by the end of Thanksgiving Day, word had gotten out to the wider world about the airplane crash. I had my fifteen minutes of fame as the story was carried around the nation by various news outlets. People from our extended family of faith around the country started contacting my parents' home, offering their prayer support and other assistance for us. In the following days, both Donna and I began to experience the power of these prayers uplifting us, almost allowing us to float above the circumstances in a miraculous way that we both find difficult to describe even to this day. I felt as if I was literally wrapped in the arms of my Lord while He was carrying me along by His strength. Our sense of God's presence was so tangible and real that Donna and I could not help but want to discuss it with each other. On one of her visits, as I began to try to describe my own experience, a smile broke out on her face. Donna then explained to me she knew exactly what I was talking about and that she also had been planning to tell me about her experience. As she spoke, she held out her left hand, palm upward, and stared into it as she made small circles in it with the index finger of her right hand. She said, even though she was traveling down a dark and unfamiliar road she felt completely safe and secure, just as if she was cradled in the palm of God's hand as He bore her along. As we compared notes, Donna and I realized we shared an identical sense of an intimate and secure connection with the Lord. And it was apparent that even the nursing staff could see something special was happening. They remarked more than once about our attitudes and behavior and the peace we seemed to have in the present difficult circumstances. I was told directly that I wasn't behaving like a "typical" multi-trauma patient, whatever that is. I tried to make a joke out of it by suggesting that perhaps it was only because I was new at this game. But there were a couple of nurses on the ICU staff, one male nurse and one female, who told me they were born again Christians. They knew exactly what was happening and their fellowship and understanding was especially sweet at this time. However, another nurse just shook her head with a kind of *now-I've seen-everything* expression on her face. She reasoned that I was only experiencing some kind of drug induced euphoria. I didn't attempt to argue with her, but I knew her explanation didn't account for Donna's identical experience. Donna and I knew the peace we felt was a gift from God and did not originate from within ourselves. We were both learning that the gift of peace from God really is a kind of—*peace that transcends all understanding*—Philippians 4:7.

Another example of the real power of prayer stands out in our memory. One prayer request was for Donna to find some kind of alternative lodging in the Winchester area rather than motel accommodations. She wanted to stay with me until I was able to be moved back to Pennsylvania and since no one knew how long it would take, the expense of a motel would likely become prohibitive. What do you do? You call upon your brothers and sisters in Christ even if you are a total stranger. Sometime on Friday, my mother began making phone calls to area churches to ask if there was someone in their congregation who could provide a room for Donna while she stayed with me. The second call she made was to Calvary Baptist Church in Winchester, pastored by John Kinzie. My mother explained to Pastor Kinzie who she was and why she was calling. Pastor Kinzie had heard of us on the local news and graciously offered a room for Donna in his own house— prayer request answered. They even gave Donna a key to their house so she could get in if they were not home or if they were in their finished basement and the front door was locked. While we were in Winchester, Donna became an adopted daughter to Pastor John Kinzie and his wife, Anne. Their graciousness and provision for Donna really touched our hearts and made a huge difference in Donna's life. Ultimately, we named our first born daughter, Charis Anne, in Anne Kinzie's honor. Charis, by the way, is the English transliteration of the New Testament Greek word that means—grace.

I was moved out of the ICU the night before Mark's funeral was to take place at home. The change to a standard two-bed hospital room was like moving out of Grand Central Station to a peaceful country cottage. By comparison, it seemed almost as quiet as the forest scene on the mountain when I first "arrived" there. I did not have a roommate on Monday, and the quiet solitude gave Donna and me plenty of time to reflect on the funeral activities that we knew were taking place at home. It was a somber and sad day for us. The move also meant leaving the ICU nursing staff who I had bonded with and getting to know an entirely new staff. I would be in this room until we left Winchester on Sunday, December 10. I had at least two roommates during this time, and at various times I pitied them because of the commotion my condition caused. Because of me, there were times they were forced to endure sleep deprivation or interruptions.

A couple of the ICU nurses came to visit me in my new room from time to time after the transfer—a kind gesture. Donna also came to visit every day, spending hours with me. It is here we began what has become a tradition for us. Donna read out loud to me to pass the time. It was out of necessity since I could not watch TV or read myself. She read James Herriot's, *All Things Bright and Beautiful*. It was a wonderful light-hearted book, each chapter consisting of a vignette taken from the life of the author. Today we still continue this practice out of pure enjoyment when either of us finds a book we'd like to share. We read it to each other before we turn out the lights at night.

After a week on the surgical floor, it was time to install me in the cast-brace. This was apparently a fairly new mode of treatment that had come out of the Vietnam experience, according to my surgeon. My surgeon decided not to operate and install plates, screws, and rods, etc. to tie all the pieces of the shattered femur together. He made this decision for a couple of reasons; the fracture was in several pieces and would require a lot of hardware and "baling wire" to stabilize and, additionally, the break was too close to the knee to make inserting an alignment rod possible. He decided to do a "closed reduction" that involved manipulating the break to align the pieces as much as possible with the aid of x-ray and without making an incision. I was taken to an operating room and sedated with general anesthesia. When I regained consciousness in the recovery room after the procedure, I had separate casts on each leg. The cast-brace on my left leg ran from my hip to over my foot and was hinged at the knee with the traction rod still exposed. My right leg was placed in a separate straight cylinder cast, from upper thigh to ankle. (Another opportunity was missed to discover the wound at the base of my spine. How was that possible?) The next day, for the first time since being hospitalized, they allowed me to sit up in a wheel chair. This turned out to be a mistake because the cast-brace shifted, causing me acute discomfort. That night there was so much pressure on my left heel, with resulting pain, that I insisted they remove the part of the cast around the heel. They complied and I experienced relief but my roommate missed some sleep due to the commotion.

The following day, approximately two weeks after I was first hospitalized, I could not ignore an obnoxious odor that seemed to be coming from me with increasing regularity. It smelled something like a ground beef package that had been in the garbage for a few days in the summer—highly offensive and not nice for polite society. I had received whiffs of this offensive odor from time to time in the early days of my hospitalization when I shifted my position on the bed. It was odd that none of the nursing staff or doctors had ever noticed or commented on it. Nor did they investigate the source of the blood stains I regularly saw on bed sheets when they were changed. But now I resolved to take matters into my own hands. When Donna was there, I asked her to pull out the mirror that was inside the bedside service table. I asked her to put it under me as I pulled myself up off the bed by doing a horizontal chin-up on the overhead bar that ran the length of my bed, from which all the ropes, pulleys, and counterweights were suspended. I wanted her to look at my backside as it was reflected in the mirror and tell me what she saw. The pain in my pelvis, hips and lower back had never gone away and I was always struggling to relieve the pressure on the end of my spine by positioning extra pillows under me and shifting my weight as much as possible. When we did this exercise, Donna discovered a deep and wide puncture wound at the base of my spine. The surrounding tissues had become necrotic; what I smelled was my own rotting flesh. Donna immediately went to the nurses' station and insisted the nursing supervisor come take a look. I repeated my chin-up maneuver. The shift-supervisor positioned herself for a direct look and then swore out loud—never a good sign when it comes from the medical staff. The nursing supervisor then called a resident doctor in for a look. I had never personally dealt with this doctor before then. During chin-up rep number three, he took a gander. The doctor wrinkled his nose just as the others had done when they were in such close proximity to the source of the offending odor after which he quickly withdrew his head and stood up. He thought for a moment, furrowed his brow, and then proffered a diagnosis; it was a bed sore. I tactlessly contradicted him on the spot and told him he was flat-out wrong. He didn't take it very well and I could tell he felt insulted by me, although that was not my intention. I was sure he was wrong because I had occasionally smelled this odor from almost the second day I had been in ICU and had seen the blood stains on the sheets from the very beginning. Also, it did occur to me that he was not about to admit the staff had overlooked this serious injury.

I can't remember how the wound was treated immediately following its discovery, but I do remember—that very night I began to spike a high fever. It's a very strange experience to be overtaken by a massive infection like that, and I grew more ill by the minute. I rang for a nurse and requested she take my temperature because I knew I was burning up. She was shocked to see it had shot up to 106 F in a matter of a couple of hours since the last routine temperature check. This started another round of frenzied activity around me, and again, I felt sorry for my roommate because of all the commotion. It was impossible for him to get a wink of sleep while I was the center of all this activity in our room. A nurse shoved an aspirin suppository into me—not the usual way I take an aspirin, but I didn't have much choice in the matter. Then I was literally packed in dozens of ice bags to bring the fever down as fast as possible. I was told this action was taken to mitigate against the possibility of the high fever sending me into convulsions. The ice bags surrounded my torso and were mounded over it. It was oddly pleasant. They also started me on a powerful antibiotic. The fever came down over the next few hours but I would stay on this antibiotic for a very long time. This wound would be very problematic during my entire hospitalization because it was difficult to keep it from becoming re-infected and there was little air to aid the healing process since I was constantly lying on it. It did not entirely heal until I was off the bed and on my feet, over two months later.

Once that crisis was behind me and I was stabilized, planning began for my transfer back to Pennsylvania where I would continue my convalescence at a hospital closer to home. But how was I to get there? A long ambulance drive was a possibility, but the general consensus was it would be too taxing, plus a nurse or doctor would have to accompany me. Bernie May, a good friend of our family, offered some much-needed assistance to solve this problem. Bernie was a missionary pilot and the executive director of JAARS, the destination I had considered traveling to after our service call was completed. Bernie was connected with many people and he reached out to a pilot and colleague in Washington, DC who could fly us back to Pennsylvania in a Beach Craft A-36. This plane was a six place, low wing, single-engine, retractable-gear aircraft that was large enough for me (on a travel stretcher) along with Donna, a pilot and co-pilot. The A-36 also shortened the trip to less than half the time it would take to drive. Consequently my doctors felt I could do without a medical person accompanying me in the plane. Our pilot turned out to be Pastor Louis Evans, lead pastor of the prominent National Presbyterian Church in downtown Washington, DC. My departure date was set for late Sunday afternoon, December 10.

When that day finally arrived, it seemed to drag on forever. The staff prepped me for my departure while it was still very early in the morning but it was later in the afternoon when we received the message that our plane was on its way to Winchester and we were to immediately leave for the airport to meet it. We said as many goodbyes as we could and thanked everyone in Winchester for all the care and concern they had extended to us. My surgeon's parting gift to me was a maximum dose of morphine so the trip would not be intolerable even if it was difficult. I fully expected, as did he, that the dose of morphine would knock me out and I would sleep through the trip, but that proved not to be the case. I was wide awake for the entire trip.

An ambulance took us to the airport but, before we left Winchester, we were given my thick medical file complete with a hefty portfolio of X-ray film to take to my new hospital. Donna and I perused this material while we were waiting for the plane to arrive at the Winchester Airport.

Mark's glasses where I found them and now

We discovered that my Winchester doctor had written a cover letter for my new doctors in Pennsylvania in order to introduce us to them. I was very pleased to see that, in addition to introducing me to my Pennsylvania doctors, my Winchester doctor had thoughtfully introduced Donna to them with comments acknowledging the strength of her character and the important role she played in my recovery. He mentioned that she would be an asset to the staff at my new hospital. It was obvious her valuable role had not gone unnoticed by the Winchester medical staff. A few weeks later I wrote a letter to my Winchester doctor, thanking him for all he did and updating him on my progress. In April, just after getting back on my feet, Donna and I traveled back to Winchester to visit the Kinzies. While in Winchester, we stopped at my doctor's orthopedic practice but, unfortunately, he was out of town and we never reconnected. (Subsequent investigation resulted in the discovery that this wonderful doctor passed away around 1983.) While in Virginia, we also made a pilgrimage to the crash site for the first time since the accident, and I discovered Mark's eyeglass frames laying on the forest floor.

Our personal Bonanza A-36 air-transport eventually arrived at the airport in Winchester. Somehow, the pilot and his co-pilot managed to shoe-horn me into the plane but it was a snug fit and no easy task since I was flat on my back on a travel stretcher with heavy casts on both fully-extended legs. Donna had purchased a number of additional pillows knowing that, due to the continuing problem with my spine, I'd never tolerate lying flat on a hard travel stretcher for the duration of the trip. My head was at the very back of the cabin and my feet were just behind the copilot seat with my stretcher resting on folded-down seats in the second and third row. Donna's seat was also at the very rear of the cabin next to my head. We took off at about four-thirty p.m., eerily reminiscent of my departure flight that started this whole saga. The flight was smooth and beautiful even if I was just barely tolerating it. I wished I was sitting in the pilot's seat instead of enduring the ride in a supine and helpless position on a travel stretcher.

The speedy Bonanza A-36 had us back at a small general aviation airport near my home town in less than two hours. My parents and another ambulance were waiting for us at this destination. I was unloaded from the plane—an equally difficult task as the loading process—then loaded into the waiting ambulance. I was then driven to another local hospital only a few miles from the airport. It would be my next hospital home for more than a month.

CHAPTER 8

MY NEW HOSPITAL HOME

*N*ow a new hospital and a new staff would have to be brought up to speed on my case and I'd have a completely new hospital environment with which to familiarize myself. I was taken to a four-bed ward, a situation that did not entirely please me.

Things got off to a rough start. My first night there was very difficult. I was in more pain than I had been in for the past three weeks. It was the only time since very early in my recovery that my fractured left leg really hurt in addition to the other pain I was experiencing. When I asked for some pain medication, I was refused. A sympathetic but powerless nurse said pain medication had not been ordered for me. She told me the hospital's attending physician, who was not actually present the night I was admitted, had failed to order any kind of pain relief for me and the staff did not seem to want to disturb him at home to write up an order for pain meds. I guess, if I had complained loudly enough, something would have been done but I just gutted it out that night. It was a long sleepless night for me, but at least the doc probably enjoyed a good night's sleep. The following day, he finally added Demerol and Percocet to my medication list.

The next day, another doctor decided to order a culture of the wound on the base of my spine after reviewing my records. The results came back fairly quickly indicating I was infected with a highly contagious form of proteus bacteria. This type of bacterial infection was typical of a wound that had been contaminated by human feces, a painful reminder of my loss of bowel control on the mountain. I was hastily moved right out of the four-bed ward where I knew I would have been a nuisance to the other patients and where fighting the pain battle in public would have been difficult. I was relocated in a special isolation room by myself. Another answer to prayer, perhaps? I was told several warning signs were taped to the outer door leading to my room. In my imagination I saw the skull and crossbones poison logo boldly printed on all of them. But at least now I had a room to myself, even if not under desirable circumstances. And since it's always harder to deal with pain when you are among strangers in a multi-bed room, it was actually a God-send to be isolated from other patients for the duration of my hospitalization. Until I was clear of the infection, the nursing staff was supposed to gown and glove up before handling me. Visitors were limited at first, and no one was allowed to touch me. All laundry items were placed in special bio-hazard bags. It all made me feel like a pariah. All nurses wore gloves, but only a few went to the trouble to gown up. The antibiotic treatment continued and I was also required to lay in a mass of Betadine foam every day.

There was a second bed in the room but it was never occupied by another patient the entire time I remained in the hospital. After Donna was finally allowed to visit, she used it when she needed to. The room also had its own bathroom and Donna also made good use of that as her pregnancy advanced. It was all a blessing. Another blessing was that, once the nursing staff realized Donna was doing an excellent job of attending to me, we were left alone, and additionally, no one attempted to enforce regular visiting hours. My visitors came at all hours and stayed as long as we wanted. The room was isolated from the rest of the floor at the end of a short corridor and I was allowed as many visitors as I desired because we were not near any other patients and could close two sets of doors, segregating us from the rest of the floor. On Christmas Day an astonishing twenty-two people were in the room with me at one time. That has to be a record at the hospital for simultaneous visitors for one person in a room.

In those days, before the daily hospital room rate was a king's ransom, the hospital would fill up on weekends and holidays as families dropped off elderly parents or grandparents for safe keeping while they engaged in plans that did not include caring for an elderly or infirm family member. I was told on more than one occasion that the entire nursing staff went to bat for me to prevent another patient from being assigned to the empty bed in my room once my infection was under control. I learned that, on one particularly busy weekend, hospital administrators wanted to put an alcoholic experiencing DTs in the room with me. Once again, the nursing staff flat-out vetoed that move and they found other temporary arrangements for the poor guy. It was the nurses who made life bearable on a daily basis. Doctors had little if anything to do with it. I did my very best to be as light a burden as possible for the nursing staff and they seemed to appreciate it and reciprocated the consideration.

The room was spartan by today's standards. There was no TV and the bed was an old-fashioned hand-cranked affair. If I wanted to change the bed position in the slightest, I had to call a nurse or someone else to make the adjustment. I did my absolute best to request those changes only when they were there for some other purpose. It was a continual battle to keep pressure off my spine. My fractured sacrum and coccyx made it feel like I was always lying on a golf ball. Donna bought extra pillows and I was arranged on quite a few to keep the pressure off my spine, but it was an uncomfortable and endless battle. Time dragged and sleep was problematic as it had been from the very beginning of my treatment until the very end—six weeks after I was discharged from the hospital for home-based convalescence. The hospital menu became boringly routine, as I experienced its repetition on a ten-day cycle. I can thank my brother, Pete, and some others for bringing in late-night pizza and other treats on several occasions. The nurses always feigned jealousy but never accepted any food when it was offered to them. I became familiar with the daily routine of the nursing staff and learned to deal with it, along with the varied personalities of the regular nurses and their weekend replacements. It was a good thing I was completely conscious and lucid because I usually had to "train" the weekend staff regarding the SOPs of my care. I wondered how they were expected to handle a patient whose ability to communicate was compromised. They were in a difficult position and did their best. I learned never to ask for anything starting at least an hour before the end of a shift and extending into the first hour of the next shift. It was always a busy time for them as they had shift-change status meetings to attend and were also trying to catch up on last minute requirements. Those requests seemed to be rarely communicated to the next shift and if they were, unless it was an emergency, I knew they would not be fulfilled for at least an hour into the succeeding shift so I just learned to live with things and work around their schedule.

One escapade I must have perpetrated out of sheer boredom stands out in my memory. I somehow convinced one of my siblings to bring in a hideous Halloween mask that had been floating around the family for years.

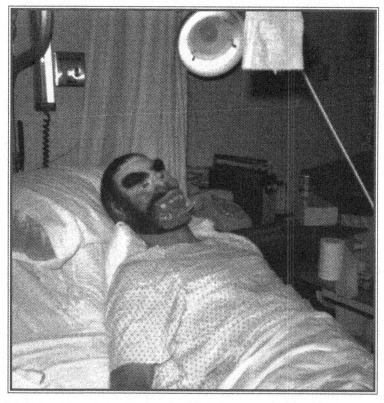

Gorilla-man lying on 6 pillows in the never-
ending battle to keep pressure off my spine

It looked like a grotesque gorilla face. One night I decided to put it on just to prank the nurses. (It *seemed* like a good idea at the time.) I donned the mask and waited for a victim. A kindly middle-aged nursing assistant entered the room but the effect was definitely more than I bargained for. At first she was concentrating on some chore that did not directly involve me so she did not look at me for ten or fifteen seconds after she came in. I just lay quietly inert in my bed. The second she glanced at me, she shrieked her loudest and ran straight out of the room, screaming down the hall. A second later, a bevy of other nurses ran into the room along with a couple of male orderlies ready for combat. None of them seemed to see much humor in the situation. Oh well. I did feel guilty about traumatizing the nurse who first saw me; that was certainly not my intention. She was a kind sort and had done me no harm. Even though I apologized profusely, she was a bit frosty toward me for a day or two. Who can blame her?

My orthopedic doctors at this hospital were not from the "cast-brace" school of medicine. They were pretty contemptuous of this approach and also claimed it interfered with the x-ray process. I was getting so many x-rays I thought I should be glowing. A few days after being transferred to the isolation room, they cut off the cast brace and it was back to just skeletal traction until a week before my discharge. About two or three weeks after my arrival, they also removed the cylinder cast from my right leg. Before this experience, if anyone had told me I'd be required to endure lying flat on my back for over two months, I would have told them I'd rather take a bullet. But, by the grace of God, I got through these things, not a day at a time, but an hour at a time.

During the first couple of weeks in my Pennsylvania hospital, I saw three different orthopedic doctors during morning rounds on a rotating basis. They were all partners in the same orthopedic practice. It was my experience that if I explained something to one doctor, I ended up having to repeat it to each of the other two on successive days. The information I passed on to one doctor never seemed to make it to the others. Finally, out of frustration, I demanded that only one of them see me. I was tired of dealing with a medical committee that did not communicate very well within its membership. One doctor in the practice drew the short straw and, except for a few instances, I dealt only with him during daily rounds for the duration of my time in the hospital.

Once I was transferred to the isolation room, one day was not much different than the next, with little variation in routine except when I had visitors. It became a matter of trying to fit into the hospital routine, bother as few nurses as possible, and just try to make it from one minute to the next, then to the next, and the next—fight the pain battle, sleeping while I could when the pain medications were at their maximum effectiveness, endure it the rest of the time—on and on.

There was one major break to the routine, however, and that was during Christmas. On Christmas Day, my entire family, including siblings, their spouses, and most of their children, plus an assortment of family friends filled my room. Everybody celebrated there with me. It was memorable. My father even brought a serving of the turkey dinner that had been prepared for the family. Unfortunately, I was dealing with more discomfort than usual on that day, but I was still happy to be included in the family's Christmas celebration. Donna hung Christmas ornaments on the various fixtures and rigging attached to the overhead support bar. I had an entire room full of Poinsettias given as gifts to me and they were augmented by those donated to the hospital by various service groups. It was a festive time with lots of laughter. I know I laughed along but my lasting memory is how bad I felt that day.

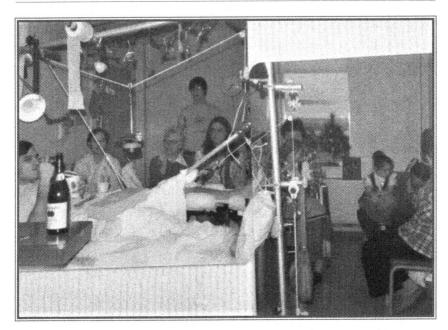

Christmastime- the only hospital photo of me sans gorilla mask. I am sampling some of the turkey dinner prepared for the family. Left to right—my brother-in-law Rick, my mother, Pete, Janet, Nancy (holding Heather), her husband Leigh (holding Chris) and Donna. People came and went throughout the day but there were as many as 22 in the room at one time.

Sometime during the second week of January, it was decided I was ready for the next phase of my treatment. The skeletal traction was to be terminated, and before discharge and home convalescence, I would be encased in a spica cast, more commonly known as a body cast. It would be a single spica, meaning only one leg would be part of the cast. My right leg would remain uncast. Happily, that meant I would possibly have the opportunity to walk on crutches even after being installed in the cast. I was told there was some debate among my doctors whether the spica should be single or double. The single spica view won the day. A nurse who had been part of those deliberations later told me she asked the doctors to "have a heart" and not put me in the double spica. The single spica was bad enough. A body cast or spica cast wraps around your entire body at the waist, starting just below your rib cage. Then the cast extends down one or both legs, in my case the left leg, totally encompassing the foot. The purpose was to stabilize my hips in addition to the femur since I had also fractured my pelvis.

I was taken down to the orthopedic casting room. I was positioned on something that looked like a bicycle seat mounted above a table, and my legs were extended horizontally in the air with my feet clamped into boot-like structures on another adjacent table. To say this was uncomfortable is an understatement. It was all I could handle because now my entire body weight was sitting on my tail bone and I'd been struggling to keep my body weight off my tail bone ever since I entered the hospital. The first order of business was to remove the threaded rod that had been in my shin since November twenty-second. It was screwed out with the same type of manually operated brace that was used to screw it in. This was not pleasant, but it was over quickly. Since the residual skin penetration wounds would be covered by the spica cast, I wondered how they would not become infected over time, but that never happened. Then various layers of leg stocking and wrappings were applied before the actual plaster. The team worked quickly but, even so, I wasn't sure I was going to tolerate the entire procedure. The doc noticed I was obviously struggling during this procedure, and judging by his expression, he seemed annoyed that I was experiencing that much pain almost two months after my accident—like it was my fault. Because of his obvious annoyance, I voluntarily reminded him, through clenched teeth, that all my weight was now concentrated on the very spot that had given me so much pain for the last two months, and I further reminded him of the unhealed wound that was still there. He actually said, "...oh, yeah..." as if he had forgotten all about those facts, but then he said it was too late in the process for any pain meds. (It's never a good thing when your doctor says "oh, yeah" while discussing your medical condition.) You see, the wound was always treated by another doc—not this guy's business. And the fractured sacrum and coccyx were things they never could address—out of sight, out of mind. You have got to love those docs.

I had a somewhat contentious relationship with the docs at my PA hospital the entire time I was there. I played no role in choosing them and they certainly played no role in choosing me. I was in this hospital only because of its close proximity to my own home. But this moment was the one time I really wanted to slug one of them. Every morning for the last month one of them would come into my room on morning rounds and ask me how my leg was doing. Every morning I would reply that my leg was fine—that the source of most of my pain was my lower back, pelvis, and spine. And every morning it seemed my comments went in one ear and out the other. As far as they were concerned, I was the guy with the badly broken leg they were treating. The doc installing me in the spica was not my morning rounds doctor so, once more, I was bitten by the lack of communication between members of the practice. Do I sound frustrated? It was also at this time that my forgetful doc casually and almost offhandedly tossed out the news that my left leg was probably going to heal in such a way that it would be about an inch shorter than my right leg. This was the first time I was ever informed that this outcome was a possibility. Now, I am fully aware this was a trivial matter compared to the medical tragedies that some have been called to bear, and I don't know why this news startled me, but it did. I guess my working assumption all along was that eventually I'd heal up and be right as rain with no lasting effects. I had always been athletically active and, until then, in good physical shape, and I had taken a bit of pride in that. I belonged to a gym and ran twenty to thirty miles a week before it was a trendy thing to do. I remember seeing case history notes a doctor had dictated at the time of his initial examination after I arrived at the Front Royal hospital ER: "...patient is a well-developed male..." Now I know this is just medical jargon describing a person with no obvious congenital physical defects, but I fantasized at the time that it was commentary on my buff, although broken, physique. How self-servingly naïve can you be? But continuing to think I was going to emerge from this ordeal without lasting complications was a convenient coping mechanism that was comforting to hold onto. I was already angry at the doc and now I was angrier at this latest news that was so nonchalantly dropped on me. Eventually, when I had a cooler head, I understood how this news could be regarded as trivial to a doctor who, in some cases, was probably required to deliver really bad news to truly suffering people.

When this ordeal was over, I was taken back to my room. For the first time in almost two months, I asked if I could be on my stomach for a while. The nurses helped me roll over. I heaved a contented sigh just to be in a different position. It was heavenly, at least for a few minutes, but then I was rolled back onto my back and I began the long battle to negotiate a bed angle that was the least offensive to me in this new plaster prison.

The next day, I was taken to physical therapy for the first time and placed on a tilting table to begin the process of having my body adjust to being raised to a vertical standing position. Over the course of the next two or three days, the table was tilted a little at a time until I was vertical. Every time they increased my verticality, I'd break out in pouring sweat because of the change in my blood pressure. I was usually in physical therapy for less than an hour at a time. When I got back to my room, I'd have to ask for a change of gown because the one I was wearing was drenched through with sweat. After about three days, I could tolerate being vertical.

Then I began standing next to my bed in one spot for a while as I supported myself on crutches. After they were satisfied I wasn't going to fall on my face, I began to take steps with crutches. During my last few days in the hospital, I crutched around the floor with a nurse's aide trailing me as often as I could cajole one into taking the time. I didn't know what she would do if I lost my balance, because there was no way she could stop me once I started to go down. I'd learn all about this in a few days.

CHAPTER 9

CONVALESCENCE AT HOME

*W*ell, the day finally came to be released from the hospital. I was to continue my recovery and convalescence at home. My wife prepared for this and rented a hospital bed that was placed in our small downstairs living room where I would spend the next six weeks. Our only bathroom and our bedroom, where Donna slept, were on the second floor. When the time came to leave, all the first shift nurses came in to say goodbye and I thanked each one for their kindness and care over the last month. I truly meant it. I was discharged on January 22nd, exactly two months to the day after I entered the hospital in Winchester.

My father came with two of his employees to help get me from a hospital gurney into the back of a station wagon for the short drive home. Our small row home was on a hill with some steep steps leading from sidewalk to porch level and into the front door. I was unceremoniously lugged up the steps by the guys and deposited on my new bed in the living room. From there I inspected my new accommodations. In a few minutes, my father and the guys left, and I was alone in my house with my wife for the first time in two months. Now it was up to her alone to attend to my daily needs. That included such lovely chores as emptying my bed pans and urinals and carrying water for washing my body and my hair. Keeping my hair clean was an onerous chore for everyone at the hospital over the past two months. At one point I even had a haircut while sitting in my bed in the hospital to help make the task more manageable.

I can't say enough about the love and patience of Donna, my wife, during the entire time I was recovering from the accident. By the time I was home, Donna was about five months into her pregnancy. I know every pregnant woman looks forward to at least some attention and TLC during an advancing pregnancy. However, Donna's pregnancy seemed almost like an afterthought to many people, as most of their focus was on me and my recovery. Donna had to deal with her pregnancy as best she could while caring for me. Meeting my daily physical needs was hard on her. Pregnancy and bed pans do not mix very well. Bed pans don't mix very well with anything! Her love got me through the toughest part of my recovery which, we would discover, was yet to come.

After the guys left us alone, we began the process of figuring out the new normal. Our small dining room was adjacent to our living room area and Donna had moved our dining room table to the far wall to provide as much space as possible for me to get into the house and to my bed. I noticed Donna had started a jigsaw puzzle on the dining room table to provide her with some diversion during the few waking hours not spent at the hospital with me. I decided it would be a good idea to crutch over to look at it. After all, I was supposed to be able to do this. I swung myself over the edge of my bed, pushed myself upright and crutched about twelve feet over to the table. I looked down at the puzzle then up again to Donna, who was standing nearby, and was instantly overcome with vertigo. I assume it was because of rapidly moving my head. I lost my balance, and in the space of a second, I went down like a felled tree. Once I started to lose balance, there was no recovering because the body cast made me about as flexible as an I-beam. Down I went with a mighty crash that shook the entire house. My head bounced against the wooden floor, and just missed a cast iron radiator by inches. It took a few seconds to determine that the cast and I were still in one piece and for the mental cob-webs to clear. Donna stood there frozen, wearing a horrified expression.

So, what were we going to do now? Donna definitely could not pick me up. My father and the guys had just left. Was I going to call them so soon, proving I was not ready to be on my own? Donna had been planning on going to the local pharmacy just down the street to fill some prescriptions I had been given. I told her to leave me on the floor and I'd think about what we were going to do. She left me on the floor with a blanket and pillow during her walk down the street to the pharmacy. When she returned, she prepared lunch and we ate it with me still on the floor. We had a dining-room floor picnic with tomato soup and grilled cheese sandwiches as the featured menu entrees of the day. As we ate, I told her I'd thought of the plan we were going to try.

I observed that I had fallen onto the oval braided area rug that was on our bare polished wood floor. I said I thought she could drag me on the area rug over to the steps leading to the second floor. She grabbed the edge of the rug, curled it in her fists to improve her grip and, sure enough, she had the strength to drag me, on the rug, across our slippery wooden floor. I was then able to maneuver myself into a position right next to the baluster rails lining the steps going up to the second floor. I grabbed the highest baluster rail I could reach while lying supine on the floor. I told my very pregnant wife to do her best to push me from behind once I had moved a little off the horizontal. I pulled myself a few inches off the floor with one arm and then lunged and grabbed the next higher baluster rail with my opposite hand. I continued lunging for and grabbing the next higher baluster, hand-over-hand, one at a time. And as Donna pushed and I pulled, I was able to continue heading toward the vertical until I was finally fully upright. I was blessed with better than average upper body strength and it came in handy here just as it had while I was hospitalized. Back then the nurses loved how I could pull myself up completely off the sheets via the support beam over my bed so they could do a sheet change-out without exerting themselves to lift or roll me. While I hovered over the bed, they whipped off the old sheets and put on new ones. In our present scenario, as Donna pushed and I pulled, I went up without being able to bend at the waist or at the knee. Once it was all over and I made it safely back to my bed, we had a good laugh and knew we had a funny story to tell. Best of all, from my perspective, we managed to solve a problem without resorting to outside help. Maybe we could handle this home convalescence phase after all.

During this phase of my recovery, we were navigating uncharted territory. There were no attentive nurses and orderlies to call upon. What I missed most, however, was effective pain management. The low-strength pain medication I was prescribed was definitely not up to the task, and living in my plaster iron-maiden proved to be more difficult than I ever imagined, especially sleeping in it. I don't naturally sleep on my back. I had been attempting to do that for the past two months in the hospital with only limited success. Being in the body cast made it much worse, however, because there was really no bed adjustment that could ever be comfortable—just less uncomfortable. A sure way to drive yourself crazy is to be in an uncomfortable position and then not be able to move out of it. My only option was to either lay down or stand up. But how long can you stand in one spot when you are dead tired? Nevertheless, several times a night, I would get out of bed and just stand in one spot next to my bed while supporting myself on crutches for as long as I could to relieve the discomfort of lying down. I had to be careful not to nod off while standing, otherwise I might end up face down on the floor. I soon found myself in a pattern where my nights and days were reversed. I would cat-nap throughout the day and lie awake most of the night. Nights were long with nothing to distract me from the pain and general discomfort that goes along with being encased in plaster. We generally kept our house temperature very low at night and I began attempting to sleep with no blankets at all in hope that the chill would numb me, making me less miserable. It was not a very effective strategy. I developed a headache and backache that became my constant companions over the next month, and my inability to adjust my position in response to basic discomfort became more problematic over time.

On the positive side, I was often visited by friends and attentive church members. Several men from the church came to help me take my short exercise walk from my bed to the rear of the house over and over again so I could begin regaining my strength. I discovered that calcium loss in my feet due to my extended bed rest caused a lot of foot pain at first. After the fall on the first day, Donna insisted I not attempt any more walking unless there was someone there besides her to trail me. Some days were better than others, and on bad days I had to excuse myself from visitors and hope they understood. Then things took a totally unexpected turn for the worse and I found myself fighting a different sort of battle than I'd had to wage thus far.

CHAPTER 10

DARK DAYS AND OTHER CHALLENGES

*O*ne evening a friend came to visit and brought some audio tapes to share that he thought were interesting. The audio tapes featured messages given by an evangelist and speaker who had made a name for himself in Evangelical circles at the time. This man claimed he was a former Satan worshiper who was miraculously saved and transformed by Jesus Christ. He claimed intimate knowledge of occult activities and of the Church of Satan in America. (His claims have been subsequently debunked and his reputation discredited.) His "ministry", at the time, was aimed toward informing Evangelicals of the danger and alleged pervasiveness of Satanism in America. The tapes focused on the power of Satan and portrayed the speaker as almost singlehandedly battling against the forces of evil, that were in his opinion, barely acknowledged by the sleeping, ignorant, weak, and vulnerable professing Christian churches in America.

During the course of my friend's visit, as we listened to a tape, very suddenly a black wave of fear and uncertainty descended over and immersed me. It was an abrupt claustrophobic and suffocating feeling like I never experienced before. I became so agitated I had to ask my friend to leave in the middle of his visit. I was consumed with a sense of hopelessness and fear verging on uncontrolled panic—as if I was being held under water unable to breathe. As time passed, I realized these feelings were not just a transient aberration and they could not be shaken off or ignored. The blackness would not leave me and the long nights became unbearable. I became fearful of even falling asleep because I experienced horrible dreams. I dreamt I was buried alive or I could not move out of a very uncomfortable contorted position. It became torture. I dreamt my discomfort and pain would never end—a version of hell.

My Lord, who until then had been my strength and my acknowledged source of comfort and grace, seemed to have turned His back on me. There were a few nights when I pleaded with Donna to come and sit with me during the night. I can only imagine how hard this was for her, but I relied on her presence and strength to pull me through and she did her best to comfort me. But I could never adequately explain to her what I was going through because I did not understand it myself.

Since sleep was impossible because of the smothering blanket of fear that gripped me, I resolved to just pray through the long hours of the night. I did not pray for myself. I prayed for everyone in my life and for their needs. I prayed for every missionary I knew. I prayed for every church member I knew. I prayed for every relative and for my parents and for my siblings and their children. Eventually, I would drift off to sleep and when I'd inevitably awake in a panic, I'd start the prayer all over again. I tried to pray as much Scripture back to God as I could remember. I tried to be as thankful as I could be for God's many graces in my life and for God's provision and for the answered prayer I had already been given. I reasoned that if Satan was perhaps responsible for this curtain of fear (God does not give us a spirit of fear but of a sound mind...2 Timothy 1:7), he'd rather let me sleep than have me pray, since prayer was a losing battle for him. This cycle continued for almost two weeks but, little by little, the blackness and fear dissipated in intensity and I finally reached the point where this malaise lifted and, eventually, largely disappeared.

During those dark days at home it did occur to me that perhaps I should call my orthopedic doctors and ask for help, possibly for stronger pain medication or some other type of medication. But I dismissed those thoughts. My past experience with doctors had instilled a prejudice in me. I believed they were totally out of their element unless they were dealing with the structural, material, erector-set parts of the body and this latest challenge did not seem to directly involve those.

Probably today, medical professionals would blame PTSD for this entire experience, ignoring any possibility of a real non-imagined spiritual component to my struggle, the origins of which were separate and distinct from any thoughts or feelings that were simply created within my own head. The concept of a personal individual God who acts with rational intent is hardly tolerated in our society let alone the belief that there is a personal real individual Satan who also acts with rational intent. Yet that is exactly the world view described in the Bible whether our culture accepts it or not. And the Bible warns us that we are engaged in a real battle. (For we wrestle not against flesh and blood, but against principalities, against powers, against the rulers of the darkness of this world, against spiritual wickedness in high places—Ephesians 6:12) I believe I had unintentionally given Satan an opportunity to play with my mind by focusing on his power. I believe that God actually allowed him to battle with me and he took advantage of my weakened physical state to instill a mindset of fear in me. I believe that God allowed it to teach me something—the extent of my dependence on Him.

I am not totally dismissing the notion of something like PTSD. I do acknowledge that, later, PTSD probably did play a role in what I would subsequently experience. For many years, I dealt with flash-back episodes that interrupted my sleep. They were always the same. I would find myself dreaming about being trapped in some confined space in a contorted, uncomfortable position that made it difficult to breathe. Eventually I'd awake in a panic, gasping for breath. Sometimes, I'd have to throw the covers off and jump up from bed to walk-off the panicky feelings before I could go back to sleep. Those types of flash-back episodes reoccurred several times a year for many years following my accident and I have only been totally free of them for the past three or four years.

We had one other mini-crisis to deal with during this phase of my recovery. This one, however, was purely physical in origin. Donna became extremely ill with what seemed to be stomach flu. She dealt with those symptoms for a day or two before I also became ill. She must have been feeling a bit better because, on the night in question, we both ate a spaghetti dinner. And, while I do not think it created the problem, I know for sure that it became the problem. That night, Donna was the first to become ill with reoccurring symptoms of stomach flu and there was absolutely nothing I could do to help her through this. Then I came down with similar symptoms shortly after the onset of her symptoms, and she could do absolutely nothing to help me. We each moaned independently in isolated misery on our separate floors of the house. While Donna contended with both nausea and diarrhea upstairs, I dealt with my own situation downstairs. As soon as I perceived the metallic taste that I knew to be the precursor of impending nausea, I crutched over to the kitchen sink and stood there waiting for the inevitable praying that nausea would be the only symptom I experienced. I could not bend down over the sink, the natural reflexive action as a full-body heave takes over. As I retched multiple times, I actually thought I was going to tear out half the muscles in my body. The cast kept me rigidly upright while almost every muscle in my body contracted in a spasmodic effort to make me bend over. It was excruciating and I held on to the sink for dear life, feeling like I was going to pass out when I experienced the tunnel vision that precedes approaching unconsciousness. But I made it through the experience without totally losing consciousness.

This is one time I did call home for help. My father's response was to bring us a bottle of ginger ale. He literally extended his arm, with the bottle, through a barely-opened front door so Donna could take it without him entering our house. In a day or two, we recovered, but we were both weak from the experience.

My father had suggested several times that I should convalesce at my parents' house rather than my own home. I guess his heart was in the right place, but I had zero interest in moving back there even on a temporary basis. I wanted to fight my battle in the privacy of my own home and with my own wife. But toward the end of my home-based convalescence, I was persuaded that a change of scenery would be good so I consented to spending a night at my parents' house. It was nice to get out and experience a change of scenery, but the sleeping accommodations were worse than my hospital bed. At least the hospital bed was adjustable to a small degree, but my father thought I could sleep in a recliner chair or on the sofa. Neither proved practical and I found it impossible to sleep at all. So, after one sleepless night in my parents' house, I was glad to get back to my own home.

CHAPTER 11

BACK ON MY FEET

I continued my walking therapy and continued to gain strength and, about five weeks into my convalescence at home, I got the bright idea I could crutch up the steps to my bedroom upstairs. I stood in front of the steep stairs, told myself it was now or never, and using one crutch under my left arm with my right hand firmly grasping the banister railing to the right, I hoisted myself up via arm strength onto the first step. I continued this process, a step at a time, pausing at each step to make sure my balance was under control. Eventually, I was standing on the second floor. I had done it! Donna was not as excited as I was over the attempt but, thankfully, she did not stop me from trying. I crutched into my bedroom and haphazardly flopped onto our bed, cross-wise at the lower end. I was on my left side for a change, with my plastered left leg cantilevered off the bed in the air and my right leg resting on top of the bed. What a serendipitous discovery! Suddenly, the uncomfortable pressure on my rib cage—a continual irritant when lying in my hospital bed—was gone, like magic. The weight of the cast cantilevered off the edge of the bed seemed to counter-balance the upper half of the cast and my body, with the net result that the upper edge of the cast no longer dug into my ribs when I was lying down. I was actually comfortable! Almost immediately, I fell asleep. I knew this is where I was going to sleep until the cast was removed in about another week. I slept cross-wise at the very end of the bed and Donna slept diagonally across the remaining space.

But I still had another challenge to face; how was I going to handle crutching down the steps from the upstairs? Standing at the top of the staircase and looking down was an unnerving experience. If I leaned forward at all, I was in danger of losing my balance completely and falling face-forward down the stairs with no possibility of breaking my fall and with the greatest possibility of breaking many other things. I knew falling forward down onto the steps would be infinitely worse than falling backward onto the floor as I had that first day home. Going down the stairs required me to place the crutch on the lower step and lean slightly forward while hopping from the upper step to the lower. And during that brief moment of transition, if I could not arrest my forward momentum, I was in danger of losing my balance. But I had to attempt it.

I asked Donna to stay behind me and hold on to my waist, pulling backward to a degree. I think we even looped a belt around my waist for her to grasp like a harness. If I felt myself tipping forward, I would yell at the first millisecond and she would pull backward. Donna was to keep herself to one side of me rather than directly behind me; hopefully, I would not fall on top of her. That was the plan.

We both screwed up our courage and took the (thankfully) metaphorical plunge. I made it to the bottom in one piece. My confidence quickly improved and I was able to make the trek downward without Donna's help after one or two assisted descents.

My new mobility opened up the possibility of using the toilet instead of a bedpan since I could now reach the upstairs. One of the more implausible remarks that came from my head doctor when he first tried to sell me on the idea of the spica cast was to insist I would be able to use a toilet instead of a bedpan. Donna and I laughed at that claim with unrestrained derision after I was actually in the body cast. It was obvious that doctor had never worn one himself even if he was a fine and experienced surgeon. The only reason it was possible at all for me was because our bathroom was small and the toilet was shoehorned into a tiny space at the end of our tub behind a dividing partition. With my right hand, I was able to grab the partition's front edge while simultaneously bracing myself against the wall with my left.

I wedged my right foot against the sink vanity in front and basically lowered myself diagonally over the commode in a rigid incline. I kept the toilet seat up and just lowered myself against the porcelain bowl to maximize my target area. It was ridiculous. Nevertheless, for me it was an improvement over the bed-pan experience, and my pregnant wife was relieved of her onerous bedpan-toting chore between floors of our house.

Two days before my cast was to be removed, however, this bathroom maneuver resulted in fracturing my cast below the left knee, another sign my doctor had no idea what he was talking about. Apparently, the maneuver put high stress on a weak point in the cast where they had actually spliced the upper part of the cast to the lower leg portion when the cast was installed. The lower half of the cast completely separated from the upper half, but stayed on my leg as my foot was part of the lower half. I was determined to just live with the situation for the last two days I would be wearing the cast. I did not much care what the doctors thought so I did not see any reason to tell them about it when it happened.

CHAPTER 12

RELEASE FROM PRISON

I was scheduled to have the body cast removed toward the end of the first week of March and I was mentally counting off the days from the time I left the hospital. The day finally came, a bit more than six weeks after I was discharged to continue home convalescence. This time, I did not need the assistance of either my father or our workers to make it down the steep front steps to the sidewalk, but I still needed the station wagon my dad borrowed for the drive to the doctor's office. I loaded myself into the open rear door of the station wagon.

Arriving at the doctor's office it began to dawn on me how shabby I looked as I crutched into the waiting room. I had not been out in public since November of last year. I was wearing an old bathrobe over a pair of old oversized pajama bottoms covering my plaster sarcophagus, and I wore one old work shoe on my right foot. If I had been pushing a shopping cart filled with empty bottles and cans that would have completed the ensemble. I had washed up as best as I could, but after being inside a body cast for slightly more than seven weeks; it was guaranteed I did not smell like a rose. A waiting room chock full of people all turned incredulous gazes toward the new entrant. I could not sit down, so I just had to stand there absorbing their stares, supported by my crutches until I was called back to the de-casting room. Fortunately the call came within about five minutes.

The technician responsible for removing the cast looked at its fractured state, frowned, looked at me questioningly, and opened her mouth to ask the obvious question. I beat her to the punch, preemptively interrupting with, "Don't ask!" She closed her mouth and did not ask. In another 15 minutes, I was released from my cement prison. I gazed down at what used to be my two highly serviceable legs. Now they were just two hairy, scrawny and scale-covered toothpick-like appendages that looked like they belonged on Kermit the Frog rather than on me. Even though I was walking quite a bit at the end of my home-bound convalescence, the months of bed rest had taken their toll. My right leg was somewhat less atrophied than my left, but the left leg only had a diameter of an average arm, or so it seemed to me. If it were not for the fact that my right leg was already my weight-bearing leg, I would have collapsed when I attempted to stand with crutches sans body cast, but I was able to transfer whatever weight was not supported by my crutches onto my right leg.

After the cast was removed, I saw the doctor for the first time since I had been discharged from the hospital. He cheerily greeted me and after a minute of small talk he said something like, "Well, I guess things must have gone pretty well since we haven't heard from you since you were discharged from the hospital..." I just blankly looked at him and said, flat-toned, "Doctor, I think that was the closest I have ever come to going completely out of my mind." He gave me a blank and uncomprehending look for a few seconds seemingly scanning my face for signs of residual looniness but said nothing in response, preferring, instead, to change the subject.

After I returned home, the first thing I wanted to do was take a bath. I would normally prefer a shower but standing in a shower and washing was not possible. Before I filled the tub, I had to make sure I could get into it. My legs did not have enough strength to support me in moving from a standing position to a sitting position, nor did my abdominal muscles. I managed to get into the tub in a standing position, but I could not discard my crutches and bend down to a sitting position. (I didn't know that shower stools existed then—go ahead and laugh!) As soon as I attempted to bend either my legs or my waist to settle in, I felt myself begin to collapse. I could not even bend far enough to brace myself against the tub sides. I had Donna move a wooden chair next to the tub with its back toward it to grasp with my left hand. She sat on the chair so it would not slide or tip. I put a crutch in the tub on my right side. With these aids I was able to arrest my descent into the tub by arm strength. Then Donna filled the tub and we both went to work scrubbing off multiple layers of accumulated dead skin, barnacles, and who knows what else. My recollection is we refilled the tub several times as I rinsed following scrubbing sessions to dispose of the flotsam. Getting up was a challenge but I was able to pull myself up using the chair back and crutch. What a wonderful feeling it was to be clean and unencumbered by 50 or 60 pounds of plaster! I looked forward to sleeping next to my wife in our own bed in our usual spots.

The next morning it was time for my usual morning ablutions so I crutched over to the bathroom sink for the morning ritual. I set aside my crutches and stood before the sink, wobbling with the effort. I turned on the water, and attempted to bend at the waist to wash my face. As soon as I leaned forward a few degrees off vertical, my torso just collapsed onto the sink vanity. I did not have enough abdominal or back strength to even bend over a sink without falling in. I completed the exercise by supporting myself with one arm and washing with the other hand, slow but eventually effective. I was beginning to grasp how much rehab I needed.

Our first family get-together a couple of weeks
after my body cast was removed

I returned to the orthopedist office about once a week so they could check on my progress but, after about three visits, it seemed to me a waste of time accomplishing nothing. After the third appointment, I stopped going and that was the last I saw of them until about a year later. Up to that point, my doctor had not brought up the subject of rehab or physical therapy so I decided whatever physical therapy was required I would have to do on my own. Perhaps if I had been more patient with my doctors, they would have gotten around to prescribing formal physical therapy sessions with a certified physical therapist. But that never happened and I never found out if it was in their plans. Instead, I showed up at the local gym where I had owned a membership before the accident, still barely able to walk without crutches a month after the cast had been removed. The gym was not part of a national chain but was locally owned and I knew the proprietor very well. When he saw me, he asked where I had been for the past five months or so. He had no knowledge of my story until then, but after he heard it, he offered the gym facilities to me at no charge. For how long was left open-ended, but I did not want to abuse the privilege. I ended up using the gym for a few weeks, during which time I could see reasonably good progress toward normalcy.

CHAPTER 13

BACK TO A NORMAL LIFE

*D*onna was in the last trimester of her pregnancy and it was time to start attending childbirth classes. I was still on crutches for the first class we attended. By the second class, I was able to hobble in without crutches. It was a short hospital-sponsored series after which we attended a much longer series sponsored by a childbirth education group. That class involved getting on the floor with my wife to help her with breathing and relaxation exercises but I had lost most of the flexibility in my knees, and I remember that getting up and down to floor level was a challenge as I was still weak. It was a good thing the class was held in a church's primary department Sunday school room; it was equipped with very low tables and small chairs for children. This lilliputian furniture helped me get up and down for the duration of the class series.

Our first child was born on May 22nd, 1979. By that time I was adequately getting around without crutches, but still was not recovered sufficiently to go back to work in our family business. Nevertheless, I had been thinking about the possibility of getting back to flying.

The FAA had been keeping tabs on me and I had received several calls from the local FSDO (Flight Standards District Office) in Allentown, requesting an interview as part of the accident investigation and follow-up. I started receiving calls from the Allentown FSDO (pronounced FIZZ-DOUGH) office even when I was still in the hospital.

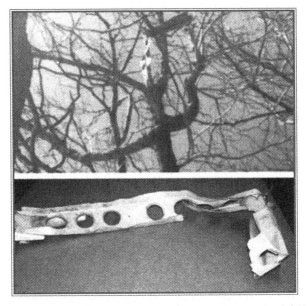

Airplane wreckage still in a tree in April 1979. It had fallen
out by the time we revisited the site, 11 years later

The first call was amusing. Someone from the Allentown FSDO office curtly said I must report for an interview within two weeks. I just laughed and told them I was not going anywhere and I had no timetable when the interview might be possible. I described my limitations to whoever was on the other end of the line and speculated that I still had months to go before I was ambulatory. Apparently the FAA does not make house calls, so they said they would check back in a couple of weeks. They were true to their word and I received a call approximately every two weeks, but after two or three calls, they became annoying. It was always the same. They were not calling to ask about my condition or progress but to restate their demand that I report for an interview. It was as if they were ignorant of my situation and the description I offered; each time was new information to them. I had to tell them in each call that my recovery was going to be an extended process and I was not ambulatory. They seemed to suffer from the same lack of communication in their office that afflicted the doctors who worked with me. Once I was back on my feet, however, an interview date was established. This was a preliminary interview that could potentially lead to a formal disciplinary hearing depending on the evaluation report submitted by the interviewer. The FAA could decide if my license should be revoked or suspended, and/or fines could be assessed should I be found in violation of the FARs (Federal Aviation Regulations) or to have operated an aircraft in a reckless or unsafe manner. It was even theoretically possible that criminal charges could be filed, not that anyone expected that to happen in my case. I had read many horror stories in various aviation publications in which pilots complained of being mistreated at the hands of the "jack-booted thugs" at the FAA, so I was not looking forward to my own face-to-face confrontation with them. Nevertheless, I determined to do my best to answer all questions truthfully and contritely and let the chips fall where they may. I had already been interviewed and had given statements regarding the facts of the accident, even when I was barely speaking on my second day in the intensive care unit of the Winchester hospital, and those statements were now part of the investigation record.

On the appointed day, I drove up to the FSDO office located at the ABE Airport in Allentown and met with an FAA examiner. It was a lengthy interview but, instead of being given the third-degree treatment by some jack-booted thug, I found the examiner who questioned me to be considerate and even sympathetic to my situation. He put me at ease. We talked at length about my entire flight experience up to the day of the accident and about the details of my last flight. The interview included an extensive and probing evaluation of my decision-making process and where I thought I had failed in that process. I could tell the examiner was looking for signs that I was unwilling to admit any culpability, but I never felt he was trying to be unreasonably tough or confrontational. And he seemed to grasp there may have been extenuating circumstances that contributed, at least in part, to the overall outcome, even if I had made some serious errors in judgment. At one point I was starting to show some emotion when discussing the death of my brother. The examiner interrupted me, drew himself closer and, with lowered voice, began a story about his own history and flying experience. Amazingly, he revealed to me, that in his past, he also had been responsible for the death of a passenger. He absolutely did not have to reveal any of his story or admit his own failure as a pilot. Nothing in his job description as an FAA flight standards examiner required him to tell me these personal facts. He chose to do so simply as a compassionate human being. I could have been interviewed by any sort of government bureaucrat but I was being interviewed by someone who had been in my shoes. I was speechless. I knew this blessing was totally by the grace of God who was still working things out in my life. I still thank him for the grace and mercy I experienced and continue to experience from his hand. The end result of this phase of the accident investigation was my license was neither revoked nor suspended, nor was I fined. I was told I only needed to fly with a flight instructor who would then endorse me as qualified to operate an aircraft and I could continue to exercise the privileges associated with a private pilot license.

Charis's birth was a happy event for us as we became new parents although, when Donna had time to reflect on her experience, her reflection provided enough motivation for her to pursue a course that would shape the next 30 years of her professional life. She became a certified childbirth educator and later she was certified as a labor and birth doula. I was at Donna's side throughout her labor to support her and to witness the birth of my daughter, although I'm sure Donna would say I did more witnessing than helpful supporting. (I did a better job of supporting her during the births of our next two children.)

A few days before, unbeknownst to Donna, I had already scheduled time with a flight instructor as required by the FAA in order to resume flying as pilot-in-command. I wanted to get back in the saddle. As fate would have it, that appointment was scheduled for May 23rd, the day after Charis was born.

That morning while Donna was still recovering in the hospital, I drove to our local airport to do some flying with an instructor as required. My only worries were how I was going to get into the airplane and how I would handle the rudder pedals. My legs were still very stiff and weak so hoisting myself up into the plane took all the lower body strength I had. It was a good thing the plane had an assist strap that I could pull on as I lifted myself up to the cabin deck level before I took the pilot's seat. Once I was in the seat, I managed to flex my knees sufficiently to swing my legs into the airplane. An airplane is steered on the ground by the rudder pedals that are interconnected to both the rudder and the nose wheel. Pressing a pedal turns the nose wheel to steer the plane on the ground in addition to displacing the rudder to turn the plane in the air. It is not power-assisted and it takes quite a bit of pedal pressure to execute turns on the ground. I managed well enough during the slow speed taxi to the active runway but it was an effort. Once I was lined up on the runway for takeoff and the plane began to accelerate, the pedal forces needed to steer the plane decreased because the rudder became increasingly effective. When the nose wheel was rotated off the ground and the plane was flying, all directional control came from the rudder. I found the pedal forces were manageable. We flew for an hour, performing various flight maneuvers, and then we returned to the airport and landed to a complete stop after completing several touch-and-goes. I expected the instructor would sign me off with just one more hour of flight review. After that happy hour in the air, I drove to the hospital to see Donna and our new baby. I could not refrain from telling Donna what I had been up to. She later told me she was not surprised by my desire to fly again, but she was surprised I had done it so soon. I received the requisite eye-roll when I told her she couldn't keep a good man down.

I flew again in a day or two and received the required flight instructor's endorsement in my log book indicating I had satisfactorily demonstrated competent airmanship and I was approved to act as pilot-in-command. There was not much flying in my near future as we were totally immersed in our on-the-job training as new parents and I was concentrating on regaining enough strength to resume work. But in time, I became fully reengaged in aviation as an active pilot and eventually earned an instrument rating so there would be no repeat of the circumstances that led to my accident.

My work involved quite a bit of physical activity so regaining sufficient strength and endurance was a necessity before I could contribute in any meaningful way. I returned to work in early June. It was difficult at first and I only put in half days for a couple of weeks, but after that I was back to a normal routine.

A view looking South toward the approach direction—
The airplane's trajectory through the trees is clearly visible

I looked back on the first day I entered the hospital after my accident. Not really comprehending the severity of my injuries at the time, I even asked my doctor if he thought I'd be able to sing in the concert in December that I had been preparing for before the accident took place. I remember the doctor giving me an are-you-crazy look and shaking his head. I asked my doctor how long he thought it would take to walk again. He could have given me an overly conservative answer so I would not become disappointed at any future slow progress, but his response was "One year." I beat his estimate by five months.

Cairn erected on accident spot during a visit in 1996

I have much to be thankful for. God has, indeed, treated me better than I deserve. Even though there were long-term effects resulting from my injuries—I had two surgeries on my right knee culminating in a total knee replacement, and I deal with chronic back pain due to severe arthritic changes, stenosis, and advanced degenerative disc disease—I consider myself to have been blessed. I was blessed to feel God's immediate presence in my life and to receive multiple and sometimes dramatic answers to prayer. I was also blessed by that relatively short flash of hopelessness when I thought God had turned His back on me—an experience that has motivated me to keep in close touch with Him since. I was blessed to have my faithful and loving wife at my side throughout the entire experience. We both agree our spirits were welded together in a way that I doubt we would have ever achieved without being forged together in the crucible of this trial. I'm grateful that she is still by my side and we can share life together. Thank you, Lord.

John Mark Lipsi
October 21, 1951- November 21, 1978

What thrilling stories ... will one day be told in heaven, where I am sure there will be endless time to trace the threads of His weaving

Inscription Mark wrote in his Bible

CHAPTER 14

THE BACKSTORY

*T*here is a backstory to this story. If you have read this far you will realize that I relate my story from the point of view of someone who has a personal, day-to-day, living, relationship with Jesus Christ. Jesus, himself, in John 3:3 described that kind of person as being "born again". The backstory answers the question—how can I claim to have a relationship with Christ or be "born again"? In fact, how can anyone? Spoiler alert—it was and is totally by the grace of God.

The purpose of sharing my story was to tell the story of God's grace in my life during one specific time period, but God was working in my life long before those events. God's grace was at work and evident by the mere fact that God had brought me into this world with parents who, themselves, had, a living relationship with Christ, and into an extended family with dozens of relatives who also were committed Christians, and into a social setting that included many others who were purposeful followers and disciples of Christ. I was surrounded by plenty of people whose relationship with Jesus Christ was the foundation on which they built their lives and whose lives were open to inspection. I was distinctly blessed to be exposed to solid Bible teaching at a very early age. But none of those advantages and blessings automatically made me a "born-again" Christian; being surrounded by other Christians did not make me a Christian any more than being in an ocean surrounded by fish made me a fish. Nevertheless, faith does come by hearing and hearing does come by means of the Word of God, to paraphrase a quote from the

Apostle Paul, and being surrounded by other Christians was the means by which I heard the Word of God.

I believe that God signed the adoption papers making me part of his family when I was a four or five year-old living in New Jersey with my parents and my older sister, Nancy. I have a memory of a morning when our family was sitting around our small breakfast table in the kitchen. My father, a young man of about thirty or thirty-one, had just completed leading his young family in morning family devotions. He had read a Bible verse and talked about it to us. I cannot remember the specific verse he shared with us that morning, although it may well have been the familiar, John 3:16. However, I do remember almost exactly what he told us and, looking back, I realize that his message was aimed directly at my sister and me. I specifically remember he said Jesus Christ, the son of God, died on a cross for my sins but that He was alive again and wanted to live in my heart so I could also live with Him and not have to die for my own sins. That is just the way my father phrased it. My father said that Jesus would come into my life and live in me and He would forgive me of my sins, if I just asked him to come live in me and forgive my sins. That was it. That was the sum total of my father's message.

Connected with the memory of those family devotions is my memory of standing in the kitchen at my Grandmother's house, later the same day. My grandparents lived only a few blocks from our own house in Audubon, New Jersey. I happened to be alone in my grandmother's kitchen. I'm not sure why I was alone in my grandmother's kitchen; perhaps I only wanted to steal some cookies from her cookie jar. Nevertheless, I also know that day I was thinking about what my father had said—I needed to invite Jesus into my life and ask Him to forgive my sins. Even as a four or five year old, dying for my own sins sounded like a very bad idea to me. At that moment I consciously asked Jesus to live in me and forgive my sins. Since then, I have almost sixty-three years of hindsight to reflect on, and I know that Jesus did answer that child's prayer at that moment.

What does a five year old know about Jesus? What does he understand about Jesus being the Son of God? Does he have any understanding of

Jesus as the atonement, or of the concept of redemption? Does he even really comprehend the nature of sin and what repentance or forgiveness really means? The simple answer to all those questions is he knows almost nothing. But I do know a five year old already understands what a guilty conscience is and he knows he has already done wrong in his life. And such is the beauty of God's plan of salvation that it is accessible to even a child. It is so simple, so very simple, that even a child can come to Christ and be accepted on the basis of his unformed, child-like, immature and nascent faith. In fact, that is exactly what Jesus meant when he said—"I tell you the truth, whoever does not receive the kingdom of God **like a child** will never enter it." There is no college degree required—not even the ability to read the Bible, no great intellect, no graduation or degree from the school of hard knocks, no measuring up, no promises of self-reform required, no deals, no negotiating, no income threshold, only total dependence on and acceptance of God's promise. As an adult, that is what it means to become "like a child"; it means you are totally dependent on what God has provided, not what you bring to the negotiating table. How many of us could ever be saved or find favor with an absolutely righteous God, if any of those other conditions were a requirement? How would we ever know if we brought enough to the table to merit or earn our salvation? God knew that salvation had to be absolutely and unconditionally free to us, even if at the same time, it was infinitely costly to Him. Such is the nature of God's grace; such is the nature of God's unmerited favor! He offers his grace to us as a gift. In fact he offers himself to anyone who is willing to accept him!

So that is the end of the story—I became a signed, sealed, and delivered Christian as a five year old boy and everyone lived happily ever after and I spent the next sixty-three plus years just polishing my halo—right?

Now if anyone who's ever known me is reading this, they are either holding their sides in laughter at that notion, or they are snickering in disgust. (There is always one in the crowd with no sense of humor.) Of course, life is not like that, even life with the Spirit of God living inside of you. We are all broken people and sometimes the cure and recovery can take a lifetime. In fact, mostly, it does. And not only are we broken in and of ourselves, but we are faced with an adversary, Satan, who, as the Bible tells us, "prowls around like a roaring lion looking for someone to devour." Therefore Christian growth is rarely a straight line, linear forward, and upward process.

But God was faithful on His part. He continued to express His grace toward me by providing everything I needed to grow and thrive spiritually. I had parents and a church family who loved me and I was in a place where God's word was honored and there was plenty of opportunity to study and learn it. Yet growing up in this kind of environment also had some unintended negative consequences. It meant I was growing up with a somewhat limited understanding of the depths of my own sin nature, a limited understanding of the consequences of sin, and a limited understanding of just how far God's grace extended in my life. There's the old adage—*familiarity breeds contempt*. During my teenage years, while I definitely wasn't contemptuous of Christ, Christianity, or the Christian "life-style" that was more-or-less handed to me, I certainly began to take it for granted. And Satan, looking for any chink in my armor he could take advantage of, found this vulnerability in me.

Now flash forward to my late teen years and early twenties. I have another distinct memory. But this memory is not of a specific time, place, or event but of how I generally felt during those years. I was in the throes of what I call, *the second generation Christian blues*. I remember an old gospel hymn we used to sing fairly often titled, *Since Jesus Came Into My Heart*. The first verse started with the bold and joyful proclamation—*What a wonderful **change** in my life has been wrought, since Jesus came into my heart!* Huh?

I asked myself—what kind of change ever took place in me? I had "accepted" Christ at an early age, to use the familiar evangelical Christian jargon, and I could not put my finger on any great outward or obvious **changes** that ever took place. I wasn't the gangster saved out of a life of crime or the drunk saved out of a life of wasted debauchery. I was just a kid who was blessed to be in a great situation. I failed to really grasp that God's grace not only can restore a life, it can also preserve a life. It not only can save *out of...* after the fact, but it can save *from ever...* in the first place. It was all the same grace, but I was blind to that aspect and dimension of it. I didn't reject Christ or the gospel message or my need of a savior during those years, but I lost my perspective and I lost what mature believers call, *the joy of my salvation.* And about at the same time, I woke up to the fact that there was an entirely different class of people in the world. I discovered that there was this breed of humans we call females, that apparently, I had always been surrounded by, but who lately, had begun to exert a strange and unfamiliar attractive force—what can I say, I was a late bloomer.

Once the dating chapter of my life story began, I discovered an entirely new battle ground and ultimately I discovered I did not have the will power to do the right thing that I thought I had or I should have. In fact, I failed pretty miserably. And as a result, I discovered firsthand why the Bible describes Satan as, *the accuser of the brethren.* Satan took my moral failure and fashioned it into a dagger that he didn't hesitate to plunge directly into my own soul. And boy, did he ever take joy in doing it; so it seemed to me. He had me convinced I was the only, so-called, Christian who was so morally weak that I failed in the first really hard sustained moral battle I ever faced. He had me convinced that I was useless to God and God was unchangeably ashamed of me. I became ashamed to let anybody know I was a Christian for fear of damaging God's reputation even further. So for a period of several years, I became what I later called "a secret service Christian". By that, I meant I purposed only God and I would ever know that I was a Christian. I hoped no one else would ever notice me. I thought I could minimize the damage I had done to God's reputation and my own sense of self-worth by just lying low, just like a secret service agent tries to be invisible, hiding in the weeds.

But God was gracious. Over time, God proved He wasn't finished with me yet. In hindsight, I now realize that God was prodding me with small bits of encouragement here and there, just to remind me that He had not forgotten about me. There were instances during this generally fallow and unhappy period in my life when, despite my attempt at invisibility, people actually took notice, that in some small but positive way, I was not acting like everybody else around me. On several occasions when I was working in industry during Drexel co-op assignments, I was approached by co-workers who actually took the initiative to ask me to explain why I had done this, or not done that. And this happened without me consciously trying to be someone, or to do anything to cause others to take notice of me. I was asked how I managed to get along with one particularly difficult person who nobody was able to work with. Once I was asked why I didn't use profanity. Another time I was asked why I seemed to have a positive attitude during a specific negative work situation when everyone else was despondent or bitter. Each time I was asked a question like that, I was dumbfounded because I wasn't consciously trying to look or act differently from anyone else. I realized I was being served up a golden opportunity to give a testimony that was honoring to the Lord. Unfortunately, I only said something wishy-washy, if I said anything at all. I resisted talking about my faith for fear that at some later time I would trip up and give God yet another black-eye. In hind-sight, even as I hid from God, He was telling me, that He still loved me despite the many real or perceived faults I had. I had to come to grips with a truth I had been hiding from. It wasn't God who had rejected me, but it was me who was hiding out from God and who was rejecting His grace and forgiveness.

Toward the very end of my senior year at Drexel, I really felt and experienced the grace of God as He lovingly pulled me back to Himself. He caused me to seriously confront my attempt to try and live a Christian life anonymously by not making any visible waves. He made me realize that the natural outcome of my "secret service" approach to the Christian life was a total lack of joy in my life. He continued to teach me the extent to which I had been forgiven in Christ. I had to make a decision, either God's indwelling of the believer is real and His grace makes a difference, or it was hogwash and just wishful thinking. Over time God told me to take a good look around at the many professing committed Christians that surrounded me. I had known most of these people my entire life and had viewed them over the long haul. I had to admit that, on the whole, they were different. Sure, they all were just regular people on one level, with all the faults and shortcomings of regular people, but there were just too many who seemed to live life on a higher and more joyful plane that surmounted those faults and joyfully forgave them in others. God was showing me that I couldn't ignore the reality of their experience and existence, even if that experience was currently something I could not claim for myself. I was tired of hiding in the weeds and I really wanted to be joyful and productive in my Christian walk. To top it off, I was asked to take on some teaching responsibilities in my church and I knew I could not do that unless I was really walking with the Lord. I had some long heart to heart prayer time with God over several weeks, clearing the slate. Then something else happened that God used to confirm He was making a change in my life. Actually a closely linked series of events took place that God used to move me to where He wanted me to be.

Less than a year after I graduated from college and was working in our family business, a missionary couple, Jack and Chic Ruth, returned to the US on their first furlough after serving almost five years abroad with JAARS. Jack was also a Drexel graduate and was a civil engineer. He used his building and design skill to great effect in Ukarumpa, Papua New Guinea. Ukarumpa was Wycliffe's main base of operation in New Guinea, where Jack and Chic had served most of their first overseas missionary assignment. (Wycliffe is actually known as SIL, Summer Institute of Linguistics, around the world, hence Ukarumpa is really SIL's New Guinea main base of operation.) Jack was formerly a member of our church. He had an ebullient, magnetic, larger-than-life personality and was irrepressibly positive in his outlook. You could not help but want to be around him. Chic, his wife, was equally outgoing and fun to be around. My parents had a history with this couple. Years before, they introduced Jack and Chic to each other for the first time. After they married, they subsequently moved to San Diego where Jack was employed as San Diego's chief city engineer with responsibilities that included oversight of San Diego's urban development building projects. God eventually led Jack to abandon his career path and go into "full-time" service for the Lord, when he learned there was actually a need for civil engineers in missionary service. But since both Jack and Chic were from southeastern Pennsylvania and they both had family here, they came back to this area to begin their furlough (home assignment as it is now called). When they arrived, neither had a current US driver's license but they needed to get down to Waxhaw, North Carolina, where JAARS is headquartered. It was decided that I would drive them down to the JAARS base in one of our family's cars. During that week long road-trip adventure, I was privileged to get to really know Jack and Chic. I also had the distinct privilege to stay one night in the home of Cameron Townsend (Uncle Cam) and his wife Elaine and to have dinner with them. Uncle Cam was legendary for his missionary vision and was founder of SIL, Wycliffe, and JAARS, an awe inspiring but totally humble man to be around—one of the giants of the modern Christian era.

As a result of that trip, not only had I been in the shadow of, and been encouraged by some real spiritual giants, but I learned that later in the summer, Jack and Chic were going to be part of a Wycliffe/JAARS delegation to a huge event to be held in Dallas, Texas. That event was called Explo '72 and was sponsored by Campus Crusade for Christ. It was a combination youth rally, a week of intense Bible study, and an organized evangelistic outreach into the entire city of Dallas. Part of the weeklong event also included a Christian job fair. A large exhibition hall was filled with Christian organizations presenting opportunities for service to graduating college students. Every night, mass rallies were held in Dallas's original Cotton Bowl, filling every seat and the entire playing field with energetic youth. The display pavilion and all the teaching venues were located at the Texas State Fair Grounds adjacent to the Cotton Bowl. Because of the time I had spent with the Ruths, Jack knew I was, at least, open to the idea of missionary service and he certainly wasn't averse to making a strong pitch. I was already a newly licensed pilot and was naturally drawn toward missionary aviation. The Bernie May of *An Appalachian Trial* was also already a family friend and had made a strong impression on me. Jack and Chic invited me to go to Dallas with them. They said it would be fun, and I could lend a hand with the Wycliffe/JAARS delegation and get to know the organization. But I dismissed their invitation out of hand and told them it was not possible because of work obligations. Jack told me to pray about it and that he and Chic would also pray about it. Be careful when people like Jack and Chic Ruth tell you they will pray for you. Things are going to happen.

Three days before Jack and Chic were to fly to Dallas, I played in a church league softball game. I was a runner on third base. The batter hit a ground ball to the infield. I attempted to score on the play. As I slid into home plate, the cleats on my right foot caught the edge of home plate as I slid in. Home plate was not securely fastened down to the ground and one edge was slightly curled up so my cleats caught it as I slid across the plate (…I was safe, by the way…). My right foot came to a sudden stop and my ankle buckled as it absorbed the full momentum of my body. I heard a crack, but my momentum caused me to immediately rise up from the slide and hobble off to the bench all in one continuous motion. I immediately sat down on the bench. While everybody around me cheered the play, I knew I was not going to finish the game. I went to the hospital emergency room after the game and my ankle was x-rayed. A radiologist was not on site that evening, but the emergency room doctor said it did not appear to him that anything was broken so he sent me home. That night I could not sleep because of the throbbing pain in my lower ankle, a pain that I would later recollect. I received a call from the hospital the next morning. The radiologist who just reviewed my x-ray said I did have a fracture in one of the small bones of my ankle and I should immediately come in to have a cast installed on my lower leg. It would be a walking cast, but I needed to have it on for four to six weeks. I complied, and came home with my leg in a cast. Then I realized I was going to miss a few weeks of work. I also realized that I was now available to accompany Jack and Chic to Dallas. Just what had Jack and Chic prayed for, anyway?

When I talked to Jack, instead of getting any sympathy, he broke out in unrestrained laughter. He thought it was absolutely hilarious how God arranged things so I could be with them in Dallas. I told him to curb his enthusiasm (in so many words) until I determined a seat was still available on the flight to Dallas. I guess I was still a doubter. A seat was available and that same day I bought tickets for the flight. On the very next day I found myself, cast and all, on a plane with Jack and Chic headed for Dallas as an unofficial Wycliffe/JAARS delegate to Campus Crusade for Christ's, Explo- '72.

Why am I even talking about this? It is because all these "unremarkable" events in my life were really God's remarkable outworking of His grace. It is because Explo-'72 was an event that God used to mark and seal the beginning of a new life for me. The environment was tremendous. The other Wycliffe people I met were awe inspiring, the Bible study was life changing and I resolved, by the grace of God, that I would no longer live my life as a "secret service" Christian. The joy of my salvation returned to me and I was a different person after that.

Over the next several years I applied myself to Bible study with the same intensity as when I pursued an engineering degree at Drexel. The summer of 1973 was spent in Norman, Oklahoma at the University of Oklahoma where I was enrolled in Wycliffe's Summer Institute of Linguistics, a preparatory course for potential missionary candidates. I was actually enrolled in a master degree program in linguistics under the auspices of the University of Oklahoma. All courses were taught by members of Wycliffe and SIL International. Even though missionary service with Wycliffe or JAARS was ultimately not to be my career path, I met many more fantastic people who encouraged my personal spiritual growth. I cannot help but name drop and mention that I was privileged to have personal interaction and spend time with Dr. Kenneth Pike, SIL International's world renowned linguistic theoretician and Nobel Peace Prize nominee, who offered me some personal life advice when I asked for his council.

After I returned from SIL, I became increasing involved with various leadership and teaching activities at my church. I also was in the process of dating my future wife and we were married in 1976. We grew together (...while negotiating a few bumps in the road heading toward marital bliss—I hope you are smiling, Dear...) and I learned to be a husband with lots of "helpful" guidance from my wife.

I was married to a woman I loved, in great health, busy at work in a growing business, busy at church and enjoying my pursuit of aviation as a pilot. I loved flying because it involved all of me, physically, mentally, emotionally, and even spiritually. I was blessed to be in a position to purchase an aircraft that I could use in our business. And we did use it for business, on quite a few occasions. And we were expecting our first child. God was good. Life was good.

I had also become reengaged in musical activities. I grew up in a musical household and played an instrument in my preteen years. But during my junior high and senior high school years, when I became interested in sports, I put my musical interests aside. My musical interests reemerged while I was in college, however, and I began playing the guitar. After college I sang in my church's adult choir. My brother, Mark, also sang in our church choir. At that time, we both responded to a general invitation to church singers to join an ad hoc community choir sponsored by Philadelphia College of the Bible. They were putting together a performance of Handel's *Messiah* to be presented just before Christmas of 1978. Mark and I began attending rehearsals together in September of 1978. We were working together and also attending weekly *Messiah* rehearsals together, looking forward to this concert to be held at Philadelphia's renowned classical concert venue, The Academy of Music. Then, on a Monday in late November, the phone rang at work.

CHAPTER 15

JANET'S STORY

*I*t was Wednesday night, Thanksgiving eve. I was in the bathtub because it was the most private place in the house and I was hiding out. I was twenty years old and, for reasons unfathomable to everyone, including me, I'd blundered into an "engagement" that was, to put it gently, a mistake. The word "engagement" is in quotes because it always felt surreal to me—much the way I felt in the recurring dream I'd been having in which I was an actor about to go onstage with a vague awareness that I didn't know my lines or even what play I was in. My not-particularly-useful response to this predicament was to spend a lot of time locked in the bathroom, using up the family's supply of hot water. That's where I was when someone knocked on the door. I called out, "I'm in the tub," assuming whoever it was would talk to me through the door or wait until I got out. Instead, my mother answered in a voice I'd never heard before. She said, "I need to come in now." Her request was unheard of in our very private household. That, along with the strange quality in her voice, told me something was very wrong. My stomach lurched and my heart started pounding. In the seconds it took to unlock the door, my mind raced, trying to prepare for bad news. In testament to my youth and sheltered life, the worst thing I could imagine in that moment was that my dog had been hit by a car. (Woody was a legendary escape artist and I lived in fear that every escape would be his last.) As Mom stepped into the room, closing the door behind her, I was saying, "Woody's dead isn't he?" Then I saw Mom's face and everything stopped. I don't know how else to describe it. I stopped thinking about the dog and the strange circumstances. The moment was just a blank space that seemed to last forever though, in reality, it was probably only a few seconds. Then Mom sank to her knees by the tub and took my hand. She said, "There's been an accident. Dan is in the hospital and... and Mark is with the Lord."

Much of that night is a blur in my memory. The moments I do remember are disconnected, like out-of-order images in a slide show. I remember my father on the phone. In my memory, it seems as if someone was constantly on the phone that night. I remember Donna coming to the house. I remember her shocked, worried face. I remember one particular moment with her; we were standing in the hallway outside my bedroom. Donna was struggling to express her conflicting emotions. She spoke of her grief over Mark's loss being overwhelmed by her sense of gratitude for the fact that Dan had been spared. Her eyes filled with tears and she whispered, "Does that make me selfish?" I told her it didn't. In my own way, I was feeling the same conflict. I couldn't yet begin to comprehend the fact that Mark was gone from this world forever, but what I *could* comprehend and what I held on to in that moment was the miraculous fact that Dan was still with us, though far away and badly hurt.

Sometime later, Donna and Peter left for Winchester. I have the sense that a number of people came and went from the Troxel Rd. house that night. I know that our pastor and his wife were there but I have no memory of interacting with them. I don't remember my mother or father talking to me directly all night, but I imagine they did. I remember Mom and Dad on the phone, trying to get information about Dan but, for a while, all we knew for sure is that he was in the ER, that he was conscious and badly injured. At one point, a friend of mine called. He was a pilot and flight instructor and he'd heard about the accident through the aviation grapevine. He offered to try to learn more about what happened—why the plane went down. I knew my friend was hurting for me and wanted to help, but I remember thinking, numbly, *who cares?* He called back later with a tentative and ultimately inaccurate theory about an empty gas tank. That speculation had absolutely no effect on me that I can recall. I now know that, in the weeks and even years to come, Dan would spend countless hours examining the circumstances and decisions that led to the crash but, for me, especially that night, those things didn't matter.

Later in the evening, it occurred to me that I should call my fiancée. I felt guilty for not doing it earlier. He was going to be my husband, a part of my family, *wasn't* he? I should want him with me, *shouldn't* I? I called him but found myself unable to tell him over the phone what had happened. Instead, I just asked him to come over. The conversation didn't go well. He was irritated. It was late. He didn't feel like going out. He wanted to know why he should drive the three miles to my house. "Just tell me what's going on," he demanded. But the more irritated he got, the less able I was to say the words out loud so I just told him, again, that it was important he come over. He grudgingly agreed, and I walked outside to meet him; the last thing I wanted was for my parents to have to deal with his clueless indignation. He came down our long driveway fast, braking hard when he saw me. As I climbed into the passenger seat, he snapped, "I'm *here*. What do you *want*?" I told him, very briefly, what had happened. I don't remember his response. I don't know if he came into the house or left. I don't know if we talked more or not. I ended my "engagement" a week later. It was blindingly obvious that it was the right thing to do. My perspective had shifted and I realized that my situation wasn't complicated at all. The accident clarified much that had once seemed hopelessly confusing.

Hearing Dan's voice on the phone is one of my clearest memories from that night. When he called from the ER, Dad took the call in the kitchen while Mom used the phone in my room so they could both talk to him. I sat on the floor in my room, listening. I remember that I could faintly hear Dan's voice—not his words, but the cadence and tone, and I felt a sharp, almost painful sense of relief because it sounded familiar. It seemed to me that if he could sound like himself, he was going to make it. I hadn't realized until that moment how afraid I'd been that he wouldn't. Then, suddenly, Mom was handing me the phone. I wasn't expecting to talk to Dan, and all I could do at first was say his name. I remember clearly his first words: "Janet, I've been thinking of you."

Those simple words were both unexpected and comforting. Thinking of me? And how could it be that I was the one being comforted here? I don't remember what I said to him in response but I hope it included "I'm praying for you" and "I love you."

I know that the accident and its aftermath still resonate in our family today, as life-changing experiences do in every family. I think that the experience bound us together in some ways and held us apart in others. My siblings and I each possessed different pieces of our collective family memory. Each of us had missing pieces in our individual narratives. For most of us, especially my sisters and I, the biggest missing piece was Dan's story as told in these pages. We'd heard some of it, mostly through Peter who worked closely with Dan for many years after the accident. But with his sisters, Dan didn't open up much about his experience and we were reticent about questioning him. None of us wanted to make him relive that night on the mountain. Dan's decision to share his story has been a catalyst for connection. I talked more with him while he was writing this memoir than I had in my entire life previously. We siblings talked more with each other. I think we talked more with our spouses and with our children as well. We combed through details, jogged each other's memories, confirmed impressions and acknowledged misconceptions. And, as always, we remembered Mark together. Some moments were painful, some were sweet and most were a mixture of the two. I'm deeply grateful for all of them.

CHAPTER 16

MARION'S STORY

*L*ooking back on my early years of marriage and parenting, it seems that I was on a mission to wear out my welcome back at Mom and Dad's home. Rick and I lived in Philadelphia but we spent a great deal of time visiting the family, enjoying the comfort and support of parents and siblings. In spite of any efforts to lend a hand with meal preparation and household tasks while visiting, I have no doubt the chaos we brought tempted those at home to either lock the never-locked doors or simply head for the hills when they saw us coming. The opportunity for our two little ones to have precious time with their grandparents, aunts and uncles and, whenever possible, coordinate with my sister Nancy's visits to provide time with their two cousins was worth the risk of frazzled nerves. I am very thankful the door of the family home remained opened and we always found open hearts and arms within.

Mark's nieces L to R- Chris, Heather
(holding Rachel), Becky

In November 1978, Rick worked at Electra Products, the family business, and drove a school bus in the afternoon. He also served in the National Guard so he was away one weekend a month and two weeks each summer. I kept busy caring for Becky, who was about to turn three, and Rachel—just nine months old. Rick's full schedule provided me with a frequent excuse to "hang out" at home, but I'm fairly sure that would have happened even if he hadn't been so busy. We loved being with the family and have many happy memories of that time. Some of those enduring memories involve the skill with which little Becky managed to see to it that Mark began his workday even later than his usual relaxed start time. She had only to approach him with a book in hand and he would succumb, always willing to spend extra time assisting in the development of her imagination. A blanket wrapped around the two of them while enjoying a story together was a boat. A pair of slippers could not possibly have been intended for the feet, anyone could see they were puppets. A sturdy cardboard box with a rope attached became a wagon for touring the yard. Mark loved to observe and imitate the developing language of all his young nieces and was fascinated by what he often referred to as their "computer brains" absorbing and processing information at lightning speed. We all loved watching Mark interact with children, all children, but especially our children. He loved them and they loved him.

I have a number of specific memories of conversations which took place in the fall of 1978 that continue to sober me. It was close to Mark's October birthday when Mom told me about a recent dream Mark had been pondering. He had described his dream to her as a train ride that took him on a journey through his life. Mom's comments to me were brief but thoughtful and I did not ask many questions. She also observed that during the days following that conversation, Mark seemed to be finding ways to stay closer. She mentioned that he was spending a little more time at home in the evenings than was his usual practice. He was helping her around the house with thoughtful gestures that were not typical, such as taking the clothes down from the outdoor clothesline and folding them. He had also tackled the project of adding insulation to the attic—a much appreciated effort though it became apparent later that it had been installed wrong-side-out. During a visit home not long after that discussion, I had some treasured time with Mark. Perhaps it was Rick's National Guard weekend because I was at the house late in the evening. Becky was just about ready for bed but was entertaining us in the heart of the home - the kitchen. Mark was sitting on the floor with her in the corner near the sink. I cannot remember with certainty what they were doing but they may have been occupied with a book. As they played, he stopped and asked me a question that went something like this. "Do you think children this age remember things into their adult lives because they have and keep the memory as their own, or because others repeat and create the memory for them?" He restated the question a second time while I mulled it over. My response was that I thought it was both. It seemed very likely to me that our childhood memories are strong impressions that are often reinforced by the conversations of the adults in our lives. We talked about visual memories, specifically remembering a person's face, also about memories of feelings, and memories of activities or events, all being reinforced by photographs and by conversation. Mark was thoughtful and continued playing with Becky until I put her to bed. We had the kitchen to ourselves and he then brought up the subject of his train ride dream. He was quiet and wanted a response from me. He asked me what I thought about it and I did not know how to answer him. The dream was clearly affecting him. I thought, but did not say aloud – *it's just a dream*. I wanted it to be just that. There were implications to this dream along with the previous conversation that I did not want to allow into my thinking. "I was on a train, watching the experiences of my life go by, my mother and father were there, then I was alone..."

Thanksgiving was approaching and we were planning our usual family gathering but, a few days before, Becky became very sick. As childhood illnesses go, this was a rough one and Becky was very uncomfortable. We dealt with sleepless nights and long days as we cared for her and worked to protect Rachel from this miserable bug. After several very tiring days, Mom suggested that we come to the house to allow her to lend a hand with Rachel and perhaps provide an opportunity for me to nap. We arrived at the house Monday, November 20, around lunchtime and quickly learned that Dan and Mark were preparing to fly down south that day to place a service call to an unhappy customer. It was not a typical event, and there was a palpable tension in the air. I felt as though we were complicating life by being at the house but I was glad for the chance to rest. I remember sitting at the kitchen table with Becky resting quietly on my lap, her head back against my shoulder, and the opposite of her usual cheerfully animated personality. Dan came into the kitchen. At that time Dan and his wife Donna lived in Perkasie so I am not certain why he was there for that short time. He stopped by the table and spoke to Becky, commenting that he was sorry to hear that she was sick. A moment later Mark came by as well. He sat down and looked at Becky and repeated Dan's words and, knowing her throat was very sore, he told her not to try to talk. A short time later I took Becky into the living room and created a nest of blankets and pillows on the floor where she could lie down. I was beside her as she dozed off. Mom must have taken charge of Rachel or she may have been down for her nap. Mark stepped into the living room and stood at the doorway, the piano to his right. He had a small package in his hand and he quietly said to me, "I have Becky's birthday present here. I wish I could give it to her now, but I think she's too sick." Her third birthday was coming up, November 27, one week from that day. I was very touched that he had uncharacteristically prepared early. He struggled over whether or not to give it to her. He said, "I don't know - shall I give it to her now – what do you think?" I said, "I think you should hold on to it and give it to her when you come home and she is feeling better." He continued to hesitate and finally said, "I'm leaving it here, you can give it to her if you decide to." He placed it behind the music stand of the piano and turned to leave. After a moment I felt uncomfortable about not actually saying goodbye to him to I went to look for him. I found him in the garage. I did not see Dan around. Mark was standing on the opposite side of his car. For some reason, in my memory, I see him holding a sneaker in his hand. He may have been getting his shoes out of his car. He stayed on the other side of the car and talked to me over the roof. I was concerned about Becky's illness and worried about contagion so I did not approach him. I told him I just wanted to say goodbye. He looked worried or annoyed, I could not tell which and then he said firmly, "I don't want to go". I really did not know what to say in response. After a moment I said the only thing I could think of since it seemed he didn't have much choice, "Well, just hurry and get it over with quickly and come back soon". We said goodbye and I think I said, "I'll see you" and I went back inside feeling as though I wanted to give him a hug but thought I had better not. Did I tell him I love him?

Tuesday, November 21, we were back in our own home in Philadelphia, Becky was improving slightly and I was focused on caring for our girls. I had a phone conversation with Mom discussing Becky's health and talking over Thanksgiving dinner plans. She mentioned that she was very concerned about the boys and wished they would call. We talked about their open-ended plans but she was still hoping for a call. I remember standing at my kitchen sink while we spoke on the phone. I suggested that perhaps their day had become complicated and the opportunity to call was somehow missed or overlooked. "They'll be back soon, Mom."

Wednesday morning I had a lengthy phone conversation with my close friend Jill. She was always reading and recommending good books. Her current book was Phillip Yancey's *Where Is God When It Hurts?*. She read a portion from one of the last chapters to me and we talked about it for quite a while. I have since read this book several times and will never cease to wonder about God's gracious preparations and the kind way He used Jill to brace my footing during an earthquake we had no idea was well underway. The section Jill read compares death and birth. As young mothers, Jill and I had often discussed childbirth. This passage describes the pain and turmoil of our birth, when we are made to move from a place of protection, security and comfort—our world literally pressing in on us with unimaginable force as we endure overwhelming, unfamiliar pain. We are pushed from safety through darkness, toward noise, cold and then blinding light. *Birth*. Comparatively, in death we fear being forced to relinquish the familiar comforts of our lives. We fear the prospect of enduring pain. We fear the unknown. But God's Word assures us that nothing about our suffering is unknown by our Savior. Jill wrote in the copy of this book, which she later gifted to me, "Jesus carries the marks of suffering..." He gave up all for us, He relinquished His glory to be born in humility in order to provide our redemption. "For unto you is born this day, a Savior..." He lived and died for us, as Hebrews states: "...but for the joy set before Him, He endured the cross and bore the shame." He endured the shame that should have been ours in order to provide a way for us to stand before the Holy Creator free from shame. He took on all this so that our death can be the beginning of life when we step into His presence forgiven and transformed by His righteousness and free of fear. His perfect love casts out fear. These were the things Jill and I discussed that morning.

Later in the day, during a phone conversation with Mom, I was reminded that she was extremely worried about the boys. She'd been trying to keep herself busy but was in a serious state of anxiety. She had done everything she could do to prepare for Thanksgiving with the help of Dan's wife Donna, including setting the table. She said she had suffered through a terrible night, but I had no idea how terrible until sometime later.

That afternoon, Rick arrived home from work earlier than usual. The expression on his face was one that I could not interpret. I was in our living room with the girls and he went directly to Becky and spoke with her quietly but firmly and said, "You stay here with Rachel, I need to talk to Mommy upstairs for a minute." He quickly ushered me upstairs. Suddenly my head was swimming, I had never seen this expression before, I felt completely confused and felt as though I couldn't hear. He held my shoulders and looked at me directly. He said quietly, "The plane went down..." I heard rushing in my ears...

"...It sounds like Dan will make it..."

"What?"

Again...

"What?" ... "Mark?"

"No"

You can feel an earthquake in your body without moving. I never knew that before.

Our next-door neighbors, Terry and Susan, were good friends from our church. I remember Terry being in our house, I remember taking a phone call from Jill in which she said, "Marion – just remember what we talked about today." I remembered.

We gathered some clothing and numbly made a quick plan. Becky would be dropped off at the home of Rick's brother George and his wife Cathy. Becky had never been away from us overnight. I could not imagine how or when we would ever explain any of this to her. I knew that could not happen right away. Rachel, still so young, would stay with us. The ride from Philadelphia to Lansdale was mostly silent, tears streamed off and on, our minds were full of swirling questions. We had very limited information. We knew that Dan was in terrible shape and had endured the entire night on a mountain with severe injuries and exposed to freezing temperatures. I thought about the anxiety Mom had experienced that same night.

We dropped Becky off with a few quick instructions. Leaving her was extremely difficult but we knew she was in good hands.

We arrived at the house. There stood Mom in the family room looking frozen. She hugged me stiffly and asked if I was okay. She was not crying. Pastor and Esther Reif were there. Difficult decisions were being made about who should travel immediately to the area of the hospital where Dan had been taken. Thankfully, Pastor Reif was able to give guidance through the emotion and it was quickly settled that Peter and Donna would travel together, leaving as soon as possible. Peter then had the fearful task of going to the hospital where Mark's body had been taken in order to identify him. This sounded utterly impossible to me as did the task that later fell primarily to him, to dismantle and remove from the mountain the remains of the plane.

As a family, we were walking through uncharted territory. Losing Mark, along with not knowing what the future would hold for Dan, changed each of us profoundly as we found our family identity redefined. At that point, we did not know what kind of battle Dan would face in the months to come. We had few details regarding what he had already endured, what the days ahead would hold for him or what level of recovery he could hope to reach. Peter also began a unique journey that night that found his life direction altered.

Mom and Dad knew they needed to wait until the following day before leaving to head south. It was decided that Janet would travel with them. At the time, Nancy and her family were visiting her in-laws in Florida, and they quickly began their drive north with the plan to stop in Front Royal, Virginia to be with Dan and those of the family who were gathering.

We endured a restless night and then, early in the morning, Mom, Dad and Janet began their trip to Virginia. It was Thanksgiving Day. I looked at the dining room table set in expectation. What a bizarre sight that was. I found it almost impossible to walk into that room. The table remained set for several days because none of us could bring ourselves to remove Mark's place setting. A dear friend from Montgomery Baptist Church had offered to prepare the turkey which was ready for the oven. She said she knew we would need food eventually and she wanted to help. She was right; it would be needed. Food was very far from my mind. Our friends found ways to care for us, binding up our wounds as they worked through their own sorrow.

One of my tasks was to place phone calls to those less likely to have received the news. Word of the accident was spreading fast without my calls but there were certain people Mom was concerned might not have heard. After struggling through just a few calls with great difficulty, I found myself completely unable to get the words out again. The person on the other end of the line repeated several times, "Just say it Marion." Shortly after that call, I remember receiving a call from someone I had never met but whose name I had heard through my brothers. Mark and Peter had met this family at a Christian conference in Philadelphia. I remembered hearing pleasant comments about time they had spent with the DeSilva family. They had seen the news report on TV and were very apologetic for the call but knew no other way to verify the information. I had no idea that night how our two families would be woven together when, a few years later, Peter would marry Deborah DeSilva. This phone call made me realize that others would have seen or heard news reports – something that had not yet occurred to me. Everything felt so surreal – even breathing.

Decisions had to be made, some of them before Mom and Dad were able to return from Dan's bedside. A service had to be planned. I remember climbing into the back seat of the fairly new car belonging to Mark's dearest friend, Ross, as a few of us headed to the local garden shop where we struggled to select something for the front of the church. I commented on a long ink mark from a pen across the new back seat. Ross's response was, "What was a source of irritation has become a fond memory." Mark often had a ball point pen in his back pocket. Ross's words came back to me later when it was discovered that the attic insulation Mark had installed, was installed wrong-side-out. No doubt, had Mark still been with us, the family would have responded differently.

At the garden shop we decided there would be no cut flowers. They just didn't seem fitting. Instead, two holly bushes and many pots overflowing with delicate Baby's Tears. There would be a very private viewing, immediate family and closest loved ones who were searching to find a way to begin a process of goodbye. How do you select the clothing for your twenty-seven year old brother to wear to his grave?

Isaiah 61:10a, *I delight greatly in the Lord; my soul rejoices in my God. For he has clothed me with garments of salvation and arrayed me in a robe of righteousness...* Mark, like me, with a collection of battles and problems, had responded to the Lord's call on his life a few years earlier. He described this event to me saying, "I felt like I was stepping off a cliff" when bowing his heart to God. He continued to fight battles, to have and create problems just as we all do but we had seen a dramatic change from hopelessness to hope. We had watched him transform from one who was often difficult to approach and frequently sullen to one who began to enjoy life with an open heart. We don't walk forward from that point in our lives without trouble or failure. We continue to confront the same temptations that called to us before God's powerful claim on our hearts, but as I remember Mark, I remember that we observed an undeniable redirection that I trust ultimately led him into the outstretched arms of his loving Creator, clothed in the robe of righteousness purchased for him.

The time came when I had to take the little package from behind the music stand on the piano and try to find a way to help Becky understand that her beloved Uncle Mark would not be coming home. Becky opened the gift, a small boxed set of four Maurice Sendek books. She looked at each book and found that as she laid all of them open side by side, we were able to read the little birthday message Mark had written to her. Mom told me later that Mark had happily commented that he would have loved a little set like this as a young child and was very pleased to have come across it. Becky loved them too. As I carefully began to explain that Mark would not be coming home, she simply told me that I was wrong and that he would be returning. I did not argue, but a day or two later, when tucking her into bed, she said to me, "Uncle Mark lives in heaven now. We will see him there." We hugged and shared tears.

We all, close friends and family, had to learn how to walk forward in our new reality. We watched Dan, with Donna always at his side, fight his way back to a remarkable measure of health much more quickly than doctors anticipated. His badly broken body began to heal and, in time, he returned to the life from which he had been removed for a painful season. We sisters, Nancy, Janet and I also found our way back to our respective paths but felt the harshness of reality very hard to accept. The question we often asked each other was, "How is it that the world hurtles forward like nothing happened?" Mom and Dad each struggled with their new journey, keeping a close eye on Dan as they and we had to find a way to hold in our hearts and minds both God's sovereign grace and goodness and the consequences of our decisions. This is a continuing challenge. Peter, from the perspective of a sister, had a unique journey. Like Dan and Mark, he had spent hours at Electra as a boy and teenager, but his passion appeared to be an artistic calling toward woodworking but now total redirection would be required. In order to close the gap that now existed at Electra, Dad asked Peter to consider returning to the shop. With the single minded intensity that has always been his work style, Peter put aside his woodworking tools and dedicated all of his commitment and energy to continuing Dad's legacy along with Dan. As an observer, it seems to me that Peter chose to invest the same passion in his work at Electra that he brought to woodworking, desiring to honor the Lord, Dad and Mark with integrity. No one does that kind of thing perfectly, but that appeared to be Peter's goal. I think that working in the family business had been Dan's goal and intended path for quite a while, but in the aftermath of the accident, we watched Peter begin a different journey. We continue to hope that in his quieter years, he will be able to unleash those creative energies once again and build beautiful pieces of art.

Mark loved the snow. We, his younger siblings, are among those who hold memories of being coaxed outside on cold, silent, snowy nights to sled on the nearby cow hills. He found it hard to resist an opportunity to be outside in the snow. One of my most treasured memories is of a snowy day when Mark came to our house in Philadelphia with the specific intention of taking two-year old Becky to the park across the street to play in the snow. We bundled her up and off they went. What felt like a long time later I watched him carry her up our front steps, her cheeks so rosy they matched the color of the blooms on my Christmas cactus.

Becky, after her snowy play-day with Mark

Mark was worried that he had kept her out too long. They had ended their snowy playtime with Becky asking Mark to push her on the swing. Each time he asked her if she was cold or wanted to stop and go in, she answered firmly shaking her head no. He finally took the upper hand and brought her back.

Monday morning, November 27, 1978, we woke to a bitterly cold day with just the perfect amount of snow on the ground. It was Becky's third birthday, one week after Mark had placed that little gift behind the music stand. Mom was the first to say that Mark had ordered snow and we all agreed. We said our temporary goodbye that day with a memorial service at Montgomery Baptist Church. I remember very little. Our thoughts were with Dan. We sang Amazing Grace. I remember the snow.

CHAPTER 17

DONNA'S STORY

*W*hen Dan asked me to add my version to his story, I did not want to do it at first. It meant conjuring up deeply suppressed hurts and feelings. But after reading a very early edition of his story, I realized I also had to put my point of view down on paper. It has not been easy. I have shed a few tears and have been putting it off, but now that I realize other family members are doing the same thing, I made a promise to Dan that I would work on it this week.

When I look back on it now, some thirty-seven years later, I can see so clearly how God's timing was so perfect, His provision so abundant, and His comforting presence so abiding. I also know now that I went through the stages of grief much differently than Dan's family, and rightfully so.

Remember, remember, remember—is it in focus yet?

It was the Tuesday night before Thanksgiving. I went to bed shortly before 10:00 p.m. I was extra tired because I was about three months pregnant. As I was getting into bed that night, I remember praying, *Lord, I don't know where they are but I put them in your hands.* Little did I know that my brother-in-law was in the arms of Jesus, probably at that very moment, and my husband of only two years was lying seriously injured on a mountainside. Thankfully, I think I slept soundly. I would need every ounce of sleep and energy for the next two days and nights.

This was in the days before cell phones, but Dan still should have communicated his plans to me better. He had told me he was flying the company plane with his brother to Raleigh-Durham, North Carolina for a business trip and then maybe, before he flew back home, he would fly south and stop in Waxhaw, North Carolina to see missionary friends with JAARS. He never clearly made this definite to me or to his father who was, at the time, his boss. Dan had not filed a flight plan either, so if he hadn't been found in the miraculous way he was, we would have had an extremely difficult time locating the wreckage of the plane. When I didn't hear from him on Tuesday, I had to assume he went to Waxhaw. But the *Lord* knew where Dan and Mark were!

Wednesday morning, the day before Thanksgiving, I was busy baking pies at home for our big dinner at Dan's parents' house. I never did find out if those pumpkin pies were any good. I remember being proud of making homemade pie crusts. Next I ran errands. I know I went to the bank and mailed checks for bills. I now see the Lord's hand preparing the way; bills had been paid and I had withdrawn some cash not knowing I would be away from home for a couple of weeks. Also, I had just been to my OB-GYN, so I would not need to do that while I was with Dan. I had my prenatal vitamins already too.

After running those errands, I went to Dan's parents' house to help get their place ready for Thanksgiving Dinner. I remember setting the dining room table and then I was vacuuming. (Was it with the infamous Rainbow?)

When Dan's father came up the steps into the kitchen, I knew by his face that something bad had happened. Dan's mother was there too, and she and I exchanged a quick glance before Dad put his arms around both of us and pulled us both into the living room. There he told us that the plane had crashed and Mark was gone but Dan was alive, but in the hospital. How can I explain how I felt? My emotions were so mixed! I was sad for my in-laws but so thankful and relieved that my husband, the father of my unborn child, was alive. Then I felt guilty for not grieving so much for my brother-in-law. I just wanted to go right away to be with Dan.

While still embracing Dan's parents, I remember crying out to God – *God, help us!* – over and over again. I did not know how to comfort them. I later learned from my neighbor that, after I left for

Dan's parents' house, the police had come to my door to tell me about the accident. I am so glad I was not there to be told by a policeman. The Lord knew I needed to be surrounded by loving family.

Next I remember talking to Dan on the phone. I guess I was still in shock and denial. I remember stupidly asking Dan, *What happened?!* What I really meant was; *how could **you** have let this happen?* I believed my husband was a good pilot! How could he have crashed the plane into a mountain? I guess I was angry too. At who or what I cannot say for sure. Certainly not Dan, it was an accident. Not God, who had seen to Dan's rescue. I felt like I was riding on a seesaw. When I was up, I was grateful Dan was alive; when I was down, I was angry. At the same time I believed in a sovereign God who had a plan for our lives and He was in control.

In a previous account of the story, I had written that I spoke with the doctor and Dan. I do not remember that now. I have it recorded that I was shocked to hear Dan's voice sounding as if he were drunk. I do not remember that part now either, nor hearing a list of his extensive injuries. Neither Dan nor I realized at that time his leg and pelvis were so seriously broken and he would not be walking again for quite a while.

I remember Pastor Reif being there at the Lipsi's house and then my parents coming to lend me my mother's car to drive down to Winchester, VA where Dan was. Peter, Dan's younger brother, and I drove down to Winchester as soon as we could get our things packed. I also remember the Youells coming to the Lipsi's house. Polly took the turkey home with her to cook.

It was way past suppertime, but no one was thinking about eating except me. I was so hungry, but I did not want anyone to know. (Remember, I was pregnant.) I felt guilty for being hungry while everyone else was grieving the loss of Mark.

I laugh now at the things I packed in my suitcase that night at 10:00 p.m. I wasn't thinking too clearly (hunger and pregnancy), but I remembered my prenatal vitamins. Not knowing that Dan would not be wearing clothes for quite a few months (oh, those lovely hospital gowns!) it seems almost humorous now that I packed shoes, slippers, pants, and shirts for him.

I am using my previously written account in order to get these details correct since I no longer recall them. I do know that the Lord protected Pete and me as we drove that late Wednesday night into Thanksgiving morning to Winchester, VA. Then we needed a place to stay. The innkeeper must have thought it strange to have two adults, one male and one female with the same last name, asking for separate rooms after 2:00 o'clock in the morning. Maybe he guessed the situation when we asked for directions to the hospital.

The entrance to the hospital was really pretty. At the foot of some steps and near the doorway stood a magnificent Southern Magnolia tree. I remember feeling as if I were just a puppet going through the motions—or like an actress in a movie. I guess it was that denial stage again; this can't be happening. I also felt a twinge of bitter-sweetness in my heart; Winchester was where Dan and I stayed the first night of our honeymoon, two years earlier. Also, I loved the state of Virginia. I had gone to college there and loved the *mountains*, of all things! I had been on Skyline Drive many times growing up, when we traveled to Texas to visit my grandparents. I guess I was asking God *why he had to crash in Shenandoah.* I love it there. Fortunately, we both still love to go camping there. We pass right by the intersection where I-66 and I-81 cross near Front Royal on our way to camp at Loft Mountain, which is much further south along Skyline Drive from where Dan's accident took place.

I do not remember who called, but Pete or I called the hospital first and a nurse was ready to take us upstairs to the ICU when we arrived. She was so kind. I recall her asking if I had ever been in an intensive care unit before. When I said no, she explained what I was about to see. She warned me that Dan was hooked up to all kinds of monitors and machines, but said not to worry. He was not in any danger and he would get better. Still, the first sight of him threw me for a loop. His face was pretty badly cut up, his nose was broken, and his right eye had stitches. Dan asked me to give him a kiss. I'm sure he had not looked at himself in a mirror yet or he would not have asked that of me. His lips were caked with blood and extremely swollen. Nevertheless, I somehow managed to kiss those lips. The facial injuries were what I saw first and most powerfully. Most of his other wounds were either internal or were covered by dressings and blankets. It is good I did not have x-ray vision. I am sure that the Lord healed up those facial wounds so quickly as an answer to my unspoken prayer.

All of this took place in Dan's "room" at 3:00 o'clock on Thanksgiving morning. His "room" was a tiny cubical separate from the rest of the ICU. This was such a blessing because we had built-in privacy. We had only been there a short time when I felt a wave of nausea overtake me. Pete wasn't faring any better. (He tends to feel faint at the sight of blood.) That was not my problem, though. I could handle that. My problem was that I was hungry! Early pregnancy and hunger do not mix well. I did not want Dan to think I was feeling sick because of him. I do not remember what I told him, but I left his "room" and told a nurse what my problem was. I told her Pete had not eaten any supper that evening either. (Remember, no one thought about food but me.) The nursing staff was so nice! There it was, 3:00 a.m. on a holiday, and they managed to scrounge up a chicken salad sandwich, some Jell-O, and a piece of somebody's birthday cake. I insisted that Pete share the food with me and then we all felt better. I do not remember where we actually ate that food. Maybe at the nurses' station; I do not think we ate in Dan's "room." I must have gone back into his room because I do remember that Dan still had enough spunk in him that night to argue with me about the location of the accident. He insisted it was in North Carolina but it was near Front Royal, Virginia. He may have been under the influence of Demerol by then, but I could not convince him he was wrong.

I do not remember going back to the motel room, but we must have. Pete and I had to drive to Front Royal to a small county hospital near there so Pete could positively identify Mark's body. I stayed in the car in the parking lot praying like crazy for Pete. He was so kind and understanding about me not wanting to go in with him. I felt so guilty about making him go in alone, but I did not think my pregnant body would be able to cope. Mercifully, he was not gone very long. I think I may have squeezed his arm and asked if he was okay to drive. He answered, yes. God had definitely answered my prayer on Pete's behalf.

Sometime later, Dan's parents arrived with Janet, Dan's youngest sister. Also arriving that day were Dan's uncle and aunt, Uncle Dom and Aunt Margie, who happened to be in the states from Brazil where they served as missionaries. I remember eating Thanksgiving dinner in a restaurant with them. To add a humorous note to a somber situation, I recall Aunt Margie telling me to order the beets. "They are good for pregnant women!" she said. It should be noted that I detest beets and since when are beets on a Thanksgiving Dinner menu?!

I have vague memories of other family members arriving at the hospital but I do not recall on what days or in what order. I do remember that visitors were limited to two at a time in the ICU and I spent a lot of time in the hospital's chapel to escape the smoke-filled lobby.

I also remember the long hallway to the ICU elevator. It was dungeon-like, poorly lit with overhead pipes. After Dan was moved to a regular room from the ICU, I was able to use a different set of elevators not in that ugly hallway.

I remember Dan played the radio in his room in the ICU. He said it helped calm him down at night after I left. (He listened to a classical PBS station out of Washington.) This leads me to another thought—where was I to stay? I could not afford to keep staying in a motel room. I remember Dan's mother and I looked in the phone book in a phone booth for nearby Baptist Churches. She bravely placed a call to Calvary Baptist Church in Winchester. Pastor John Kinzie happened to be in his office. (I believe this was on Friday morning.) He was meeting with a couple who were to be married the next day. He told us to come right over to the church and he would talk with us. After we arrived, my mother-in-law told him that I needed a place to stay (she had already told him who we were on the phone. He had heard about the plane crash as almost everyone had by now.) He picked up the phone and called his wife, Anne. I heard her say, "Of course!" when he told her my situation. I do not remember when I went to their house, but it was so wonderful to have a real home to go to after being in Dan's hospital room all day. The Kinzies even gave me a key to their front door so I could get in late and not disturb them even though they were usually downstairs in their family room in the basement. Anne usually would fix me a cup of tea and insist on "fussing" over me. The Kinzies were so kind and hospitable. I tried not to take my usual long showers (they only had one bathroom), but I know I stayed under the shower long enough to do a lot of crying and praying. They cooked special meals for me too. (Anne kept reminding me that I was eating for two!)

I guess it was on a day that Dan was having procedures done (because I know I was not able to be with him) when Pastor Kinzie took me with him to visit a friend who, it turned out, worked in a historic house from the Civil War era. It had been turned into a small museum. It was very interesting, but Dan would have loved it much more than me. I know Pastor Kinzie was trying to distract me from worrying about Dan. It worked to some degree. Both he and his wife, Anne, were such a blessing to me. Pastor Kinzie also visited Dan in the hospital and, of course, had his congregation praying for us. I remember attending one Sunday morning service. I can also remember washing dishes at the Kinzie house one day and noting that Anne needed more dishwashing liquid so I bought her some at a nearby A&P. Looking back, I guess I could not have been at the hospital with Dan 24-7, so it is really wonderful that I had a substitute family to be with. God was and is so good! Now that I really think about it, I think Anne Kinzie washed some of my clothes for me too. I really was their "daughter" for a while.

Back to Dan—now out of ICU into a room with a roommate. (I think we mostly ignored him. He was less successful in ignoring us.) Dan and I tried watching the Army-Navy game, but the TV reception was very poor and Dan could not see much with only one eye, so we took up reading—I read out loud to him. (Obviously, he could not read to me then.) I do not recall when or where I got the book, but it was a perfect selection for our situation. James Herriot's *All Things Bright and Beautiful* had just the right amount of light-heartedness, and was divided into conveniently short chapters.

I do not remember what day Mark's funeral was, but I do remember, once again, feeling so torn in different directions. I wanted so much to be with Dan's family to comfort them in any way I could, but I also knew that I needed to be with Dan. I felt a sense of guilt once again for not grieving for the loss of Mark in the same way as the rest of the family. I had to keep telling myself that my feelings were okay. I was only a sister-in-law for two years. I had not known Mark before dating Dan. I also knew that Dan was on his own guilt-trip and I was not sure how to go about helping him. One thing I knew for sure, though, was that we both felt God's presence with us. It was as if we were both enveloped by the Lord's strong arms and were being carried along, almost on a cloud. We were both very aware of this sensation and spoke about it with each other. We both came to the conclusion that it was the result of Christians praying for us.

Dan remembers better than I what day he asked me to look at his backside. He claims I used a mirror, but I remember him lifting his body up off the bed via his "trapeze" and the overhead bar that it hung from so I could lean over and take a look. Well, once again, it is good I do not faint easily because the combination of sight and odor that I encountered could have knocked me down. I think I told Dan something like, "Okay, I'm getting the nurse!" I proceeded to the nurses station, got the attention of the head nurse and told her "Follow me!" and "You've got to see this!" Dan lifted himself up again, the nurse looked and let out an expletive. She was gone in a flash. After that, I do not remember what else happened. Dan covered that in his story. All I know is that over the next few months, that wound became part of the story of how I earned my honorary nurse's degree!

Dan thinks I bought him extra pillows while he was hospitalized in Winchester, but I remember buying pillows for his flight back to Pennsylvania. The hospital was already giving up some sheets and hospital gowns for the trip home, so I do not think they were keen on giving us pillows too. I know that Pastor Kinzie drove me to the department store in Winchester where I bought at least three bed pillows.

I do not remember much about the flight back to Pennsylvania. I know it was very cramped in the plane's cabin with Dan on a stretcher. I remember Dan's father being at the airport with the ambulance crew who transported Dan to his new hospital.

The initial entrance into Dan's new hospital is a blur in my memory. Maybe I went home while Dan was being admitted. I vaguely remember

DANIEL LIPSI

I visited a crowded ward before he was blessedly moved to a private room. We were all (Dan and I and his family) anxious to get Dan into a different room. The Lord answered that request by having that wound on Dan's backside become so infected that it caused him to be put in isolation. Hooray! As it turned out the isolation room was very private with its own bathroom and another bed which I boldly took as mine. If I had to be pregnant and at my husband's bedside as much as I was, it was great to not have to go far to use a bathroom or take a nap. The room was also large enough to hold twenty-two people on Christmas Day and the staff let me stay long after visiting hours were over at 8:00 p.m.! I usually stayed until at least 10:00 p.m. so that after my short drive home I would be tired enough to just go to bed. I did some work on a jigsaw puzzle first, which later resulted in Dan's downfall—literally!

I remember Dan getting very bored with the food and menu selection at the hospital. We all (family and friends) brought him cereal, pizzas, fruit, etc. I sneaked in extra vitamin and calcium pills.

Whenever I could, while I was there, I would try and help the nurses with Dan's care. Dan was very good at lifting himself up off the bed so we could change his sheets as quickly as possible. The nurses really appreciated the extra hands, but actually it was Dan I was doing it for. If I hadn't been there, the process would have taken much longer, causing Dan more discomfort.

Dan did not mention it in his story but I remember an issue that seems humorous now. It was recommended by the dermatologist who treated Dan's puncture wound, that he use an inflatable circular pillow under his tail bone. This was to allow air to get to the wound more easily and to take some pressure off Dan's tailbone. We were told that the "doughnut," as it was affectionately called, was currently being used by a little old lady. The hospital only had one doughnut! How could Dan take it away from a little old lady? And he wouldn't be able to give it back since it would be contaminated from his wound. I do not remember for sure, but I think somebody (I or another family member) finally purchased our own "doughnut" for Dan.

Christmas was definitely challenging for Dan but also for me. I remember being at Dan's parents' house where it seemed like everyone was just going through the motions. It felt to me like someone had thrown a wet blanket over our normally festive family Christmas get-together. I confess that I secretly resented all the attention Dan was getting while I and my pregnancy were almost ignored (at least on Christmas Day). I know I wore a maternity top and pants but I didn't really need them yet. I think I went home Christmas Day and night and had a pity party. I cannot remember when my OB-GYN appointment had been, but I do recall how happy I was to hear the baby's heartbeat, but so sad that the baby's father was not with me to hear it. I wished so much that Dan could go with me to my doctor appointments, but of course, he could not.

Finally the day was approaching when Dan was to leave the hospital and finish recuperating at home. All I can remember now is that I insisted he be in an electric bed. His bed at the hospital was an old-fashioned manual-crank type. I think Dan's father arranged for the bed we used at home. I remember some discussion about Dan going to his parents' house. Dan and I both vetoed that. We were still fairly newlywed (the two year anniversary was in September) and we wanted our privacy. Our Perkasie row house had a smaller living room and a larger dining room. The living room had a door to the front entrance hallway which we could shut, and pocket sliding doors into the dining room that we could shut. This set-up was perfect for Dan's new bedroom. I moved the sofa into the dining room to accommodate Dan's hospital bed. There was also a deep window-well in the front porch window that easily held all of the house plants that people had sent to Dan while he was in the hospital. We could also close that window shade and curtains. I remember also having a metal cart with wheels that I could push from the kitchen into Dan's room. This was especially helpful when Dan wanted his hair washed, which was more often than I cared to do, but his hair was extremely oily. Oh, and he needed to shave. I hauled dishpans full of water from the kitchen sink into the living room. Bedpans had to be carried upstairs by me to our only bathroom. Even though Dan tried to cover the bedpan contents with baby wipes and Lysol spray, my pregnant body kept me gagging through the process. (That's really when I earned my honorary nursing degree!) I would spray perfume on a scarf and tie it over my nose and mouth, but still gagged. I was so glad when those days were over!

Another way I earned my nursing degree was when I had to treat Dan's still-infected puncture wound. The nurses kindly gave me an entire unopened stack of Chux disposable pads to use under Dan's backside. Before Dan could use a bedpan, I would tape Chux pads along the edges of his body cast that were anywhere near his buttocks. Afterwards, I would remove them and clean his puncture wound by pouring peroxide into it. Next I would spread a clean Chux onto the bed and spray a large pile of Betadine foam (it looked like mustard-colored whip cream) onto it and Dan would literally lower himself into the foam. This was done every day. I remember joking that it was getting us ready for baby poopy.

Speaking of baby poopy, it was during this time that my sister started leaving her five-and-a-half to six-month-old son with me when she went back to work. I do not think it was every day, but it was a fun distraction for Dan and me. One time, after I had just given Kevin a bottle, Dan wanted to hold him. Dan playfully raised Kevin up over his head as he lay on his bed. Sure enough, Kevin spit up directly into Dan's mouth! Dan knew not to do that when our own baby came along.

The winter that Dan was in his body cast was a brutally cold one. In fact we just now, at this writing, broke or tied records from the same year for cold temperatures. Our old row house in Perkasie was toasty warm from gas-heated cast iron radiators, but water pipes in the basement decided to freeze. I remember Dan's brother, Pete, thawing them out with my hair dryer and putting insulation on them. Fortunately they did not burst.

Another weather-related incident happened while Dan was still in the hospital. It was a Sunday morning. I was trying to drive to church on an ice-covered street in Perkasie when I totally lost control of my car. The car started sliding straight for a telephone pole. I cried out, "Lord, no!" and immediately the car spun around and away from the pole. It ended up facing the wrong direction in a ditch on the side of the road. No one was around. I was not hurt. I had bumped my belly against the steering wheel, but not hard. Fortunately, I was not far from home because I had to walk back there to call the church. I do not even remember by whom or how my car was recovered and brought back to the house. I do not think it was damaged at all. How I thanked the Lord for protecting me.

Another problem that arose, and that we sort-of solved, was itching. Dan's cast made it hard to scratch an itch and his skin underneath the plaster was getting dry and scaly. We ended up putting baby powder down the cast, covering rulers and clothes hangers with handkerchiefs and then forcing them inside to try to scratch the itch. Sometimes it worked.

Pain always seems to intensify at night and that seemed true with Dan. He had a very difficult time at home without shots of Demerol or even Percocet. Darvocet just did not work. If Ibuprofen had been available then, I think it would have been the best for him but, alas, it was not available. I do not think Dan's doctors had a clue what he was experiencing pain-wise. He had such a hard time sleeping at night and he wanted me to stay downstairs with him on occasion. My bed was upstairs and my pregnant body needed sleep. I tried to stay up late with him, but I just could not. My parents lent us their little black & white TV set, but the rabbit ears antenna on it did not begin to bring in the Philadelphia stations clearly way up in Perkasie. Dan has since explained to me, and readers have already read about the claustrophobia and fear he felt, especially at night. Actually, that problem continued to haunt him for many years, only fairly recently resolving.

I do not remember anything about when Dan got the body cast removed except that after he was home, he needed my help to bathe. This was March and our baby was due in May, so my pregnant belly was now pretty large. I remember laughing at Dan's toothpick-skinny, scaly legs near my big round belly as we maneuvered him into the bathtub and began scrubbing in earnest. I wish we'd had shower gel and poofs back then. Hard water, bar soap, and dead skin made for major bathtub scum. We changed the bathwater several times. I think Dan was torn between wanting to stay in the tub and wanting to sleep on his stomach in his own bed.

Once Dan was finally lying on our bed upstairs, I took a good look at his broken-down body. I think I got angry again but, of course, I did not let Dan know this. I was remembering how we used to go bicycle riding together. Now he could hardly move. He had been in excellent physical shape before the accident. Now it was like his body had gone from that of a healthy, fit 30 year old to that of a crotchety 60-something. I mourned the loss of my husband's size 33 trim-cut and did not want to embrace the new 36 wide-bottom body. It was because of his broken pelvis that his hips became wider, not weight gain. In fact his legs were skinny toothpicks now. Over time of course, Dan's legs became strong and muscular again, but he was never the same. It took me a long time to accept that. Then of course, I would feel guilty for having those resentful feelings. I was *grateful* that I still had him alive with me, but I wanted his former good body back.

After Dan got the cast off and right before our baby was born is all a blur in my memory. I know we took childbirth classes and I finally felt like Dan could pay some attention to me instead of me to him.

I also remember that I did not like it when Dan started going back to work. I had grown so accustomed to him always being there in the house, but I had a new baby to take care of now so I stayed busy. It was not long before I was putting Charis in the upstairs window well to see Daddy's train coming up the track bringing him home from work and that is a good memory.

ACKNOWLEDGEMENTS

Thank you, Pearl Shrack, for planting a seed in me. It only took about forty-nine years for that seed to germinate, but it is directly related to this writing project. I ran into you many years after my high school graduation at a concert in which my wife and I participated as singers. When you greeted me after the concert and we both happily recognized one another, you mentioned a descriptive paper I had written in your class more than twenty years prior. That shocked and surprised me. You asked me if I had ever written anything in the years after high school. Over twenty years after that first post-high school encounter with you, your question actually gave me the courage to begin this project. After all, if my English teacher could stand reading and actually remembered something I had written so long ago, maybe I could do this.

A thank you is owed to Bernie May. You not only instilled in me an interest in aviation, but over the years, your witness and your own writing have been a continual inspiration. Thank you for reviewing this work and encouraging me to move forward with it.

Thank you to my high school classmate, Connie, or Connie-of-the-North as I like to call you. Perhaps you thought it strange that I asked you to review and comment on the early draft of this account. We had only recently become reacquainted through social media after many years out of touch. But you were the first non-family person who saw it. While I sensed this project was something that could be helpful to you at the time, I also genuinely needed and wanted the perspective of someone who had absolutely no knowledge of the story to critique it with fresh and unbiased eyes. You were kind enough to invest many hours, I'm sure, to review it in great detail and offer good suggestions, many of which I incorporated.

Thank you to my sisters, Nancy, Marion and Janet, for your

contributions of personal recollections. By the time a reader finishes this story, they will know who the real writers are in the family. Thank you for seeing enough value in this project to put yourselves back in time and relive a painful chapter in your own personal histories. And, Janet, you went far beyond the call of duty to become my go-to editing partner as you took on the roles of editor, proofreader and quality control consultant for this story as it continued to develop. Your finger prints are all over this project. And thank you, Pete, for sharing your personal recollections via our discussions. They not only gave me fresh insight into events beyond my personal experience but also helped corroborate my own recollections.

And, finally, I would also like to thank my wife, Donna, for your love, patience, and encouragement. Not only did you live through the events of this story with me, but you were forced to relive them as I committed the memories to writing. The hours I spent laboring over this story were hours I was not devoting to something else—such as working on your honey-do-list. Additionally, as the project progressed and I realized I wanted to include your perspective and experience as part of the overall story along with the perspectives of my siblings, you bravely committed yourself to that task. Donna, your encouragement also directly led to my effort to actually publish the account for wider distribution beyond our immediate family. I am so grateful that God brought us together. I love you!

Printed in the United States
By Bookmasters